SCIENCE OF HADITH

WRITTEN BY **QAZI FAZL ULLAH**

HUND INTERNATIONAL PUBLISHING

LOS ANGELES, CALIFORNIA

2024

FIRST PRINTING: 2024

ISBN: 978-1-970049-71-8

EDITED BY EVELYN THOMPSON

HUND INTERNATIONAL PUBLISHING
LOS ANGELES, CALIFORNIA
PRINTED IN THE UNITED STATES OF AMERICA

TABLE OF CONTENTS

PREFACE

Allah (Subhanahu Wa Ta'ala) the Almighty created the universe and honored humanity by subjugating it to them to utilize it for their good. Allah has also made another world for humankind, the Hereafter, with which they will be rewarded if they have pleased Allah in this world.

How can they please Allah?

Allah has sent his messengers and prophets for guidance. He inspired them and revealed to them the rules and laws. If humanity follows these laws, it will please Allah the Almighty. These prophets and messengers were not only intended to convey the Message or only to teach, but they were the perfect role models for their followers. To obey and to emulate these prophets and messengers is the ultimate success and will please Allah greatly.

These messengers and prophets were extraordinarily transparent in their nature to receive the Message and extraneously powerful in practicing accordingly. They were authentic in their words and practices, and their followers were bound to follow them. As a conspiracy, some non-Muslims and so-called Muslims tried to confuse Muslims about this proven authenticity of the prophets. However, Allah has taken the responsibility to protect and preserve the *Wahi* with all its kinds.

Allah said in the Holy Quran:

> *"Verily, it is We who have sent down the "Zikr" and verily We will guard it." (15:9)*

7

The scholars of *deen* strived hard not only to preserve the *Wahi,* but they countered this conspiracy and defeated the conspirators. Still, these conspirators are trying in one way or the other to have their goals achieved.

This Book is a series of lectures in this regard and we named it as *The Authenticity of Hadith* or Science of Hadith May Allah make it the Guidance for all! Ameen

INTRODUCTION

In the Faith of Islam, Muhammad (Peace Be Upon Him) occupies a pivotal position as a Prophet and Messenger of Allah. It is one of the essential articles of faith for Muslims to believe in and abide by all that the Prophet said or did. In *Islamic* terminology, his actions and utterances are called *hadith* and *sunnah*, respectively, which are thus, of great importance and relevance for *Muslims* of all times and places. *Hadith* and *sunnah* amplify and elaborate *Quranic* precepts to serve as precedent. The esteem for *Prophet Muhammad* does not hinge on personality cult or idolizing him. In fact, Muslims cannot profess or practice Islam without drawing upon the examples set by him. *Hadiths* are collected in the Arabic language, but translated into other languages for the benefit of those who do not understand Arabic. These are arranged by subject matter.

Hadiths are of two types, which are Sacred *Hadith* and Prophetic *Hadith*. Both types of *Hadith*, Sacred or Prophetic, are subject to the same stringent rules and standards of soundness, good, weakness, or of doubtful authenticity. *Tawatur*, depending on whether they comply with the rules and standards under which these are collected, tested and written, hands down sacred Hadith through centuries in the revealed wording of the Arabic language.

The Holy Quran states:

> *"Take whatever Prophet gives you and refrain from whatever he forbids you." (59:7)*

9

Believers have assiduously collected details about the life of Muhammad, his utterances, actions, matters, and methods of approval and disapproval. This collection serves as an elaboration or supplementary details to divine commands contained in the Holy Quran. Thus, there is an extensive thesaurus (concordance) of such information called the *Sunnah*. Apart from conveying the Divine Message, Muhammad was a social reformer and spiritual mentor. He brought about moral transformation and spiritual regeneration. He imparted instructions in every walk of life, illustrating the Divine commands and prohibitions practically to instill the conviction of commitment by influencing the human mind and actions, and he achieved astounding success.

The Holy Quran says:

> *"We raised among the unlettered people a Messenger of their own, who recites His revelations to them, purifies them and teaches them the Book and Wisdom (Sunnah), and surely, in the past they were in the wrong." (62:2)*

> *"We send down the Reminder to you (O Muhammad) so that you may explain to people clearly what was revealed to them so that they may ponder upon." (16:44)*

> *"We have sent a Messenger amongst you from your own rehearsing Our Signs to you, sanctifying you and teaching you the Book and Wisdom, which you did not know (before)." (2:151)*

His wife, *Sayyidah Aisha*, is quoted that the life of *Muhammad* is the practical demonstration of the teachings of *Holy Quran*. He is a role model for Muslims of all ages in matters of faith, morals and manners, socio-political ideas, thought patterns, concern for the hereafter, and spiritual outlook. The Prophet had overflowing love and affection for the poor, orphans, elderly, women and children. He skipped meals to feed the needy. He led a frugal life in order to better help the poor and weak. He practiced forgiveness, even though he was persecuted for many years.

He visited the sick, attended funerals and consoled the distressed. As the head of household, father, husband, and neighbor, he was an excellent example to fulfill these familial and social roles.

His commitment to fairness and social justice for all and his modesty and simplicity reflected in his repeated directives that he may not be idolized or extolled. He took great pride in being only a servant of Allah for preaching and promoting Islam, high morals and superb conduct at both individuals as well as collective levels. Some of his directives dealing with the articles of Islamic Faith are unique to the Muslim community.

For example, the *Holy Quran* demands liturgical prayer services. Prophet Muhammad is the one who illustrated all of the aspects of this command about the times, place, the number of units, rituals, and method of offering. It is through his example that Muslims realized the blessings of prayer and its role in molding their outlook on life. His utterances thus set forth the agenda for professing and practicing Islam.

Most of his directives are equally valid and relevant for non-Muslims as well, who may be struck by the catholicity of his mind and his genuine concern for the welfare of humanity at large.

His directives in the real-life situations were carefully observed and faithfully followed by his companions (Sahaba) to be emulated by the subsequent generations. Thus, this will explain the high place of his practices and utterances. Of all the Messengers of Allah, Muhammad holds the distinction of being the last and final Prophet. More significantly, he is the only Messenger whose entire Prophetic career is meticulously preserved in writing. All that he said, did, approved or disapproved of, even his slightest gesture and body language, is on record. From the very beginning of his mission, a host of his followers devoted themselves to faithfully recording his utterances and practices and transmitting them to posterity. With the passage of time, this exercise extended in depth and breadth.

Hadith sciences were soon developed and became one of the most extensive branches of learning in the Islamic tradition. Some of the best Muslim minds collected, edited and promoted *Hadith* studies. This trend continues up to this day, and it has contributed much to the popularity and importance of the utterances of the Prophet among Muslims across the world.

The Prophet was constantly under the direct care and supervision of Allah while engaged in the Prophetic mission. He was inspired and guided by Allah in all of his thoughts and actions. Thus, Muslims are duty-bound to follow his directives, in addition to those ordained by the Holy Quran. The Divine revelations constitute what we know as the Quran, whereas the special knowledge divinely imparted to the Prophet is reflected in his actions and utterances. It represents what the Holy Quran calls *"wisdom."* Imparting wisdom is specifically and recurrently mentioned in the Holy Quran as part of his assignment:

> *"...Allah has revealed to you the Book and Wisdom, and He has taught you what you did not know (before)." (4:113)*

> *"And remember the verses of Allah and the Words of Wisdom that are rehearsed in your homes. Certainly, Allah is ever so Subtle and All-Aware of all things." (33:34)*

This *"wisdom"* signifies the words and actions of the Prophet. It will explain why it is so important to learn and act upon these words. Allah both sanctions and sanctifies the path of Prophet in Surah An - Nisa:

> *"And whoever opposes the Messenger (Muhammad) after the Guidance is made clear to him, and he follows the path other than that of believers, We shall leave him with his choice and land him in Hell and that is the worst destiny." (4:115)*

12

Islamic history will corroborate that these rulings, directives and utterances of the Prophet in deciding matters in all aspects of their lives have guided Muslim rulers and citizens alike. This is still true for the Muslims of today.

A serious attempt has been made here to present a mostly faithful translation of the Prophetic utterances from the Arabic. This translation is done by the concept, rather than word-for-word. At times, the import of his utterances has been paraphrased, without deviating from the original. It is our hope that all readers, Muslims and non-Muslims alike, will benefit from it.

SACRED HADITH

(HADITH - E - QUDSIYYAH)

The authority of the Sacred *Hadith*, unlike that of the Prophetic *Hadith*, is traced back to Allah. Allah communicates a Sacred *Hadith* to the Prophet as revelation, inspiration, dreams or through the medium of the Archangel Gabriel (*Jibril* in Arabic), which he taught to people in words that the Prophet felt appropriate. The Holy Quran is, thus, superior, as its wording is restricted to those of the Preserved Tablet, which has remained unchanged ever since. A Sacred *Hadith* is sacred because of its text from beginning to end or by the presence of a phrase within the *Hadith* that is sacred.

A Sacred *Hadith* is not acceptable for recitation in the prayer services, nor may it be touched or read by the one in a state of ritual impurity or by a menstruating woman. For details, see the works of Hanafi jurisprudent, *Al Mulla Ali Ibn Muhammad Al Qari* (died 1016 after *Hijra*).

The subject matter of the Sacred *Hadith* is restricted by its nature and by the limited number of such *Hadith*. Divine utterances by which they are uniquely characterized are confined to particular domains. However, they could be grouped under the following main headings:

i. Monotheism, revealing the unique qualities of perfection and sublimity of the Majesty of Almighty Creator, and rejecting polytheism and skepticism.

14

ii.   Religious Rites and Rituals and supererogatory works.

iii.   Standards of morality and virtue.

iv.   Dedication in the path of Allah.

v.   The Day of Reckoning, with its rewards and punishments.

In general, the Sacred *Hadith* clarifies the meaning of Divinity and servitude to Allah, particularly in the fields of belief, worship, and day-to-day conduct. The style of Sacred *Hadith*, in keeping with the subject matter, mostly takes the form of direct expression. It is invariably sublime, spiritual and deeply moving. Thus, authors of the books of *At Targhib Wa At Tarhib* (encouragement and admonitions), those of devotional and mystical works quote them frequently. It is from Sacred *Hadith* in matters relating to religious Rites and Rituals, acts of virtue, repentance and righteousness.

This translation of the 40 *Hadith* follows the same procedure as adopted in the collection of *Forty Hadith* by *An Nawawi*. It provides a readable English rendering to serve as an introduction to the devotional literature.

PROPHETIC HADITH

(HADITH - E - NABAVI)

Some collections of the utterances of Prophet were edited and compiled in the early history of Islam. The most popular ones are as follows:

SAHIH AL BUKHARI

This was compiled by Abu Abdullah Ibn Ismail Al-Bukhari (810-870). He was of Persian descent, blessed with a strong intellect and a sharp retentive memory. He is considered as one of the towering scholars of *Hadith*. *Sahih Al Bukhari* contains a careful selection of 7,275 thematically arranged utterances of the Holy Prophet, sub-divided into 100 sections organized in 3,450 chapters.

SAHIH MUSLIM

This is another major *Hadith* collection by *Abu Husain Asakir Muslim* b. *Hajjaj* (817-874), next to *Sahih Bukhari*. He traveled widely, to Persia, Iraq, Syria, and Egypt to master the discipline of *Hadith*. After examining a large number of the utterances of the Prophet, he selected 4,000 authentic reports.

SUNAN ABU DAWUD

This was compiled by *Abu Dawud Suleiman Ibn Al Ashtah* (817-888). He pursued the study of *Hadith* in Arabia, Persia, Syria and Egypt. *Sunan Abu Dawud* retains the meticulous standards of scholarship found in the works of *Bukhari* and *Muslim*. However, some scholars do not regard some of the reports in this collection as reliable. Abu Dawud, however, points out the defects in such reports.

JAMI TIRMIDHI

This was compiled by a student of *Abu Dawud*, named *Abu Isa Muhammad Ibn Isa* (821-892) who continued the work of his teacher and spiritual leader. He learned *Hadith* at the doorsteps of *Bukhari* and *Muslim*. His labeling of reports as genuine or otherwise is one of the most valuable elements of his work.

SUNAN OF NASAI

This was compiled by *Abu Abd Al-Rahman Ahmad Ibn Shuaib Al Nasai* (827-915). He studied *Hadith* in Central Asia and visited Egypt and Syria for collecting *Hadith*. His *Sunan* is a large collection of the utterances of the Prophet, which is one of the six standard works on the subject. It contains variants of many *Hadith* reports, followed by the comments of Nasai on the authenticity of each report.

SUNAN OF MAJA

This was compiled by *Abu Abdullah Muhammad Ibn Yazid*, known as *Ibn Maja* (822-887). For the study of *Hadith*, he visited Persia, Iraq, Syria, Arabia and Egypt. This collection contains 4,000 utterances of the Prophet arranged in 32 sections and 1500 chapters.

SUNAN OF BAYHAQI

This was compiled by *Abu Bakr Ahmad Ibn Al Husain*, known as *Bayhaqi*. He learned *Hadith* under many eminent scholars. His *Sunan* stands out for its thematic arrangement and its method of treating Hadith reports.

MUWATTA OF MALIK

This was compiled by *Malik Ibn Anas*, who was a distinguished jurist and *Hadith* scholar of Medina. His collection of Hadith, *Muwatta* also contains the rulings of Madian jurists. His work is one of the earliest extant writings on *Hadith* and Jurisprudence.

SOURCES OF KNOWLEDGE

Humanity is proud of its intellect. We rely on it, and most people, who are involved in the material world a lot and are impressed by secular sciences, reject and refuse anything that is beyond their intellectual approach.

Is intellect the ultimate, utmost, and last source of knowledge?

Does it make sense to reject, ignore, and deny whatsoever is beyond its approach?

SENSATION AND SENSES

Animals, including humankind, are often said to have five senses. These senses are:

a)   Sight, in the eyes.

b)   Hearing, in the ears.

c)   Smell, in the nose.

d)   Taste, on the tongue.

e)   Touch, and this sense is in the whole body (some parts of the body are more sensitive than others).

Certain senses are stronger in some animals than others, sometimes even more than the human beings. Some animals do not have sense(s), but they qualify that need of theirs in another way, like a bat that comes out in the dark and flies. Its vision is poor, but whenever it goes towards a wall, for example, uses echolocation to determine where it is so it can avoid it. Now, it is a known fact that all these senses have limits. They cannot perceive beyond those limits, but still things and issues are there, and they need to know it as their life is based on its knowledge. So all animals have been given five other senses, and these are:

AL HISS UL MUSHTARAK

Its literal meaning is the common sense, as it senses all the findings of the senses described above. Those five senses pass its findings to this sense that is there in the first half of the first part of the brain, which is the closest to the forehead.

AL KHIYAL

This faculty is there in the second half of the first part of the brain, i.e., next to the previous common sense. This faculty is the storage of the findings of common sense.

AL WAHM OR IMAGINATION POWER

This faculty has the sense of things other than the subjects of the senses described above, like fear of predators. This fear is the feeling of this faculty. Its center is the second half of the middle part of the brain. However, it is spread out over the whole of the brain.

AL HAFIZAH OR MEMORY

This power is there in the first half of the third and last part of the brain. It is the storage of the findings of Al Wahm.

AL MUTASARRIFAH / AS SULTANA

Its center is the first half of the middle part of the brain. However, like Al Wahm, this is also spread out to the whole brain. It is the power that carries out the findings of Al Wahm and Al Khiyal, as if, for example, a goat sees a lion. Its shape is there in its Al Khiyal naturally, and this fear is there in its Al Wahm and Al Hafizah. So the Al Wahm and Al Khiyal both use this power of the Al Mutasarrifah. It carries out the job, conveys the message to Al Mutasarrifah, the moving power, which mobilizes and activates the goat's muscles and the goat runs to protect itself. If the Al Mutasarrifah has been used by Al Wahm, then that is called Al Mutakhayyilah. If this power is utilized by the intellect of a human, then that is called *Al Mutafakkirah* or thinking. However, in most people the *Al Wahm* overtakes the intellect and thinking and then they believe in superstitions. Only the people with a firm belief and a strong will can counter these superstitions.

THE SKETCH OF THE BRAIN

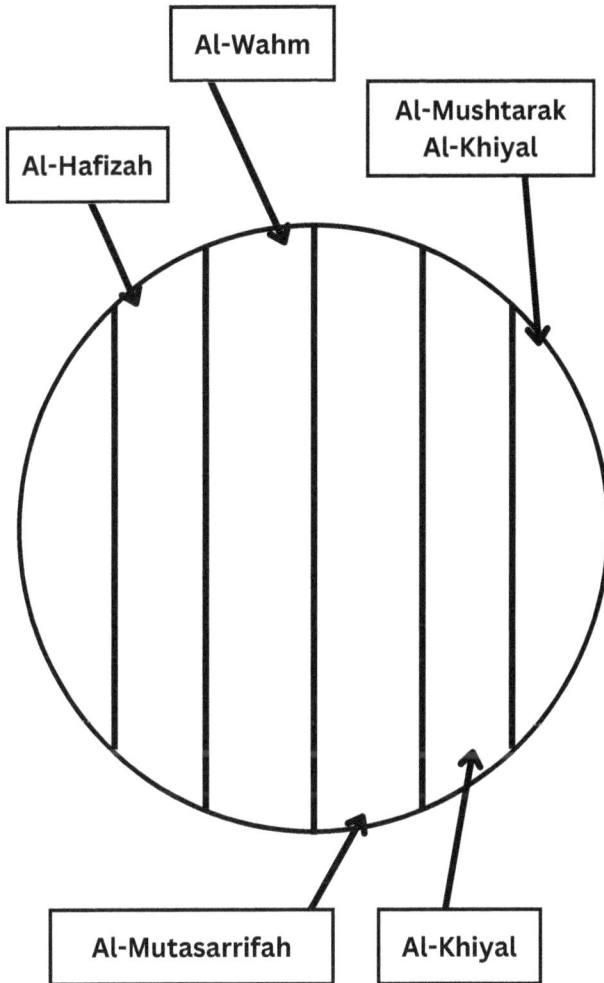

Al-Wahm

Al-Mushtarak
Al-Khiyal

Al-Hafizah

Al-Mutasarrifah

Al-Khiyal

Animals have a power called *Al Muharrikah* or the power that mobilizes.

This power has two functions:

i.   CAUSING POWER

ii. PRACTICING OR DOING POWER

The former mobilizes the latter to move and do. This power makes the muscles relax or contract. If this push is to intended to achieve a thing, then this power is called *Al Quwwat ash Sha'hwaniyyah,* or desire. If this push is to intended to repel a thing, then this power is called *Al Quwwat al Ghadabiyyah,* or anger.

Humankind, as animals, has all these senses, powers, and functions. As we see, however, they use animals, and all that is there in the heavens and on the earth, because of some other quality and sense. Allah has blessed them with a second source to understand. This is called *Al Aql,* and it is the intellect.

Let us examine this sense, where it is located in the human body, its field and function. Also, let us see if there is any other source and means of knowledge, and how important it is. This is known that humans have this second source known as intellect. It is a very transparent sense in the human body neither visible nor physical. However, it has a function and power. This power and sense are there in the human brain, and that is why sometimes the term *"brain"* is also used for this sense.

Imam Abu Hanifa and many other scholars have embraced this concept. *Imam Shafi* and some others said that intellect is in the human heart. They took various verses of the Holy Quran literally, wherein the understanding, thinking and, pondering is attributed to the heart and, all these are the functions of the intellect, so it means that intellect is there in the heart.

Allah said:

> *"They have "hearts wherewith they understand not."*
> *(7:179)*

24

"Their hearts are sealed up, so they understand not." (9:87)

"Therefore their hearts are sealed up, so they understand not." (63:3)

"So they may have hearts wherewith they understand." (22:46)

Verses like these attributed understanding, which is the function of intellect, to the heart. They also say that certain other things are the functions of the heart, like belief and disbelief, hatred, love, greed, grief, joy, etc.

We say this attribution of understanding to hearts is metaphorical, as heart is the fountain center of energy and power, but intellect is in the brain. There are many examples of this figurative attribution in the Holy Quran as Allah said:

"And We sealed up their hearts so they hear not." (7:100)

Here the hearing is attributed to hearts and nobody says that hearing is heart's function.

"But it is the hearts which are in the breasts that grows blind." (22:46)

Blindness is attributed to the heart, but the heart's function is not to see, so how it could grow blind?

"They are deaf, dumb and blind, so they do not understand." (2:171)

The ears, tongue and eyes, however, do not have the function of understanding. Also, Allah the Almighty, when mentions his Grace towards humans, said:

"Verily, We have created men from mixed semen in order to try him, so we made him to be hearer and seer." (76:2)

The animals are also created from that mixed discharge, and they are hearers and seers as well. However, human's special honor is understanding, so by this hearing, seeing, we can mean that they understand. If both groups try to understand one another, then there is no difference. Since the second group also says that the power comes from the heart to each organ and part and it is so to the brain and then the intellect works. The metaphysicians said that intellect has four categories, and one has it gradually.

These are:

AL AQL UL HAYULANI, OR THE INTELLECT IN ITS INITIAL STAGE,

This possessed by every human possesses from birth and even in utero. At that stage, it is a blank slate that will evolve later on to a level where things can be traced and printed on it. This is also called *Nafs* (self).

AL AQL BIL MALAKAH (THE INTELLECT)

At this stage a child now has the talent to understand in a practical sense. The procedure of intellect at this stage is that it goes from general concepts towards theoretical and subjective things, so it needs thinking, guesswork and hypothetical approach. The development of this phase starts in the early part of childhood and becomes mature with the age of puberty and on the basis of this intellect the *Sharia* makes humans bound to believe and practice accordingly.

AL AQL BIL FIL (PRACTICAL INTELLECT)

This is when the intellect in the previous stage develops an intuitive knowledge of things. It achieves the intellectual sciences, and those sciences are imprinted upon it. Then this intellect does not require any new effort to gain these sciences, but it brings it forth whenever it wants.

AL AQL UL MUTLAQ (A PERFECT INTELLECT)

At this stage, the intellect has achievements in its approach to things in the palm of someone he looks at it, and he can take from it whatever he wants even the whole of it. Regarding a particular science, one can have this stage of intellect in this world. However, regarding all sciences, one will have it in the Hereafter. Some scholars say this can happen to certain people here in this world also. They think of different things simultaneously and being in one situation does not get them involved totally. He cannot think of another thing because this type of intellect is connected to the spiritual world and has become remarkably transparent, which gives it extraordinary power. This last intellect is named *Al Aql Ul Mustafad.* It should be called *Al Aql Ul Mustafeed,* the acquiring intellect, as *Mustafad* is the quality of its findings which means *"the acquired."*

NOTE 1: The intellect in its second stage/category is *Al Aql Bil Malakah.* It can achieve any theory it wants without further thinking, but only by its immediate mental approach (which is called *"Hadas"* and its approach is very swift). Then this power is called *"The Holy Power"* or *"Power of Holiness."*

NOTE 2: Here are two terms: (1) *Al Fikr,* and (2) *Al Hadas. Fikr* literally means thinking. The metaphysicians said that when thinking, one goes from results towards the causes and causes towards the results. This is called *Al Fikr.* In *Al Hadas,* one moves based on one's observation and other findings towards its basics. Humans have two powers: (1) comprehension and understanding, (2) motion, practice and action. Both of these powers can be either natural or intentional.

The sense of intellect understands the rules and puts things together to achieve the desired result(s). The power of practice mobilizes the body through thinking or observations or experiences as the case may be, based upon opinions or beliefs related to these actions. So a person has two things: the desire to achieve and the anger to repel.

One is bound to balance one's powers, understanding power or practical power. If one can polish and balance his natural power, that is called *"Wisdom."* If one polishes and balances his practical power, that is called *"Justice."* Polishing and balancing desire is called *"Chastity."* Polishing and balancing anger that is called *"Bravery."*

So the human intellect comprehends the basic things and puts these accepted things to know about the unknowns. That is called *"knowledge."* It proceeds very swiftly from the basic towards the unknown, gaining knowledge and then expressing it.

The scholars also said that human intellect has two approaches, and these are natural, so a normal human has both. However, if someone becomes unbalanced s/he will be ruled by one and not the other. These two approaches are:

1. The approach to the life of this world, which is physical and material;

2. The approach to the hereafter, which is the metaphysical and spiritual approach.

Both approaches demand effort. If one makes the required effort, one will achieve the desired result. But the intellect cannot illuminate itself. Otherwise, it will be the cause and the result of itself, which is illogical. Therefore, it needs something else, and that is revelation. Because when a heart believes in a particular issue and is beyond the approach of senses and intellect, then the intellect is confused. As a result, the heart agitates and looks towards senses if it could support the idea, and that was the case when Abraham asked Allah:

"O my Lord! Show me how you give life to the dead?" (2:26)

So Allah asked him:

"He said, "Do you not believe?"

He replied:

"Yes (I do), but to get my heart satisfied."

Same was the case with Prophet Musa (Moses) when he said:

"O my Lord, show me (yourself) so I may see you." (7:143)

Moreover, he did not have the power to see Allah, so Allah told him:

"He said, you can never see Me."

The scholars also said that intellect has two aspects:

i.   SENSATIONAL INTELLECT

This is the common one. Its function is to analyze a thing or issue, explore it, and try to find out the secrets of the thing or issue. It looks for proof and clues. This is the scientific approach of the intellect. Also, the human mind is not satisfied with loose parts, so the intellect puts parts together to make it one entity.

ii.   INTUITIONAL INTELLECT

This intellect is developed through many efforts if an intellect worked in materials a lot; its intuitional approach is to the matter and material world. However, if it worked a lot in the spiritual world, then its intuitional approach is to the spiritual world, to metaphysics and the world of models. It is not satisfied with simply asking,

"What is the function and functional limits of the sensational intellect and why?" Rather, it works on "What should be its function and functional limits?"

This intellect has two fields for its approach:

1. The world of models, i.e., the nature of a thing;

2. The ultimate reality and how to get in touch with it.

This intellect tires of the material world very quickly and looks for the ultimate *"Best"* to contact that ultimate reality, which is Allah.

It has two fields of study:

i) *Sharia*, and

ii) Mystic (*suluk*).

How do we get in touch with the ultimate truth and reality?

Through symbols and rites, the most important of which are:

(i)   The House of Allah,

(ii)   The Messenger of Allah,

(iii)   The Book of Allah (the Holy Quran),

(iv)   Prayer

Being in this material world and being more influenced by matter and worldly attachments, most people have totally ignored their spiritual side. So in their contemporary liberal and secular approach, they are of the view, to understand the world without the concept of God, and they insist upon rationalism and naturalism. So they created an emotional prejudice against God, spirituality, and metaphysical affairs.

But their system is based upon neither rationalism nor naturalism, but rather upon senses, desires, and necessities. They do not give any importance to such a thing that cannot be quantified. If there is no material advantage, anything beyond observation and experience is not important to them.

Decision-making in secularism is based upon necessity and situation and not on norms and values. Its educational system is based on matter and materials, which create desires and approaches to what is good for humans, which has a philosophical reason, proven with experience, having a material advantage. The human self is the judge of the decision. Its base is selfishness and power and the way towards that decision.

DISTINCTION OF INTELLECT

DISTINCTION OF HUMANS FROM OTHER ANIMALS BASED UPON INTELLECT

A feature of humans that sets them apart from animals is their physical structure.

Allah said:

> "Verily, We have created Man in the Best Stature (Mold)." (95:4)

Also, after mentioning his original creation from clay, and then his generation from semen of male and female and giving him a beautiful structure and features,

Allah said:

> "And then brought him forth as another creature (wonderful stature). So Blessed is Allah, the Best Creator." (23:14)

Humans have three other qualities that distinguish him from other animals:

1. Animals have their physical needs and desires, and they do struggle to fulfill them. Humans also have intellectual requirements. So they look for a better way of life, a good society, and also how to avoid the punishment in the Hereafter.

2. Animals struggle to have their needs like food fulfilled, but humans want more: they want their food to be clean, pure, and delicious. Animals simply look to fulfill their sexual desires, but humans look for a loving and loyal spouse. Animals simply look for shelter, but humans want a clean, beautiful house with lots of amenities.

3. Animals are satisfied when their needs have been met. However, humans try to get their needs met in a more efficient way, where they can get more with less effort. Some humans invent things to make fulfilling their needs easier or more efficient, and others put their trust in these inventors and follow them to use their inventions.

To express the same in Sharia terms, we can say that the inventors are the inspired people, and all others are their *muqallids* (followers).

WAHI OR REVELATION

This is the third source to seek and get knowledge. However, what is *wahi*, how does it come to the Messenger, why it is needed?

Wahi means a swift indication or hurry and haste.

This is used in the meaning of:

1. On natural Instinct as Allah said:

    "And your Lord inspired the honeybees [put in their nature])" (16:68)

2. On the meaning of indication:

    "Then he came to his people from worship place and told them by sign to glorify Allah praises in the morning and in the afternoon." (19:11)

3. On the meaning of whispering:

    "And verily the devils whisper to their friends." (6:121)

4. On the meaning of bad inspiration:

    "And so we have appointed for every Prophet enemies – devils among mankind and jinn [demons] inspiring one another." (6:112)

5. On the meaning of *"assigning tasks"*:

"And he assigned in (to) every heaven its task." (41:12)

6. On the meaning of good inspiration:

"And We inspired the mother of Musa [Moses]." (28:7)

Technically this means the revelation of *Allah* to a Prophet and Messenger by an angel, either in the inscribed shape or the uninscribed, or the inspiration of Allah to him without angel. Several Messengers received written Books, while some of them received a Scripture but also verbal instructions from an angel, which were then inscribed.

Allah said:

"Verily, We have inspired you (Muhammad) as we inspired Nuh [Nuh] and the prophets after him, and we have inspired Ibrahim [Abraham], Ismail [Ishmael], Ishaq [Isaac], Yaqub (Jacob) and "Asbat" [the 12 sons of Jacob], 'Isa [Jesus], Ayub [Job], Yunus [Jonah], Harun [Aaron] and Suleiman [Solomon] and to Daud [David], We gave the "Zabur" (Psalms). Moreover, (We inspired to) Messengers We have mentioned to you before and Messengers we have not mentioned to you, and to Musa [Moses] Allah spoke directly." (4:163)

Most of these Messengers received *wahi* verbally while some others received it in an inscribed shape, which means that *wahi* is of two types:

1. Where the words and meanings both are revealed to the Messenger, and this is called *wahi jali* or Manifest and an evident revelation.

2. Where the sense and subject are revealed to the Messenger, and he conveyed the same in his words, that is called *wahi khafi*, hidden or secret revelation.

There are the three sources for seeking knowledge.

These are mentioned in the Holy Quran:

"And do not follow what you have no knowledge of. Verily, the hearing, the sight, and the heart, of each of those you will be questioned (by Allah)." (17:36)

It is the literal meaning of the verse. However, the explanation *"the hearing"* means the divine news that is *wahi, "the sight"* means whatever is known by senses, and *"heart"* means the intellect.

Also, Allah said:

"Verily in this there is an admonition for him who has a heart or gives ear, and he is a witness." (50:37)

Here in this verse also, the technical explanation is that *"Heart"* means intellect, *"ear"* means listening to the revelation and *"he is a witness"* means the use of senses.

Allah said:

"And of Mankind is one who disputes about Allah without knowledge or guidance or a Book giving light." (22:8/31: 21)

Here also, technically we say that *"knowledge"* means senses as these are the Basic source of knowledge, *"guidance"* means intellect, and *"Book giving light"* means revelation.

WHY WAHI IS NEEDED?

As we said before, that intellect is the special sense given to the human beings that made them the honored creatures, able to use and exploit the world and things therein. Its approach is vast, which is why humans need *wahi*. He may follow his intellect and believe in it as the ultimate source of knowledge, and that is what the secular philosophy says, i.e., follow nature and intellect and nothing else. However, culture is based upon neither nature nor intellect. It is based upon apparent senses led by desires and necessity. Just deny, or do not give any importance to, that which cannot be measured or has no material benefits therein. Even the very entity of Allah is not important, as it is neither seen nor can one take it through scientific experiment.

i.   As we said before, humans have intellect and that intellect has its field, approach, and limits. However, sometimes a person is not satisfied even though they have a lot of material things and physical comforts.

Why?

Because when one looks for a thing naturally or practically and he cannot get it, then the stress overtakes one.

Now when one is under stress, it means that one's nature feels short of something. Then one thing is that every living entity struggles for its existence and tries to stand still forever, and as a natural law and procedure it cannot do so. Based on intellect, one tries to get in touch with an everlasting entity to get satisfied regarding this demand of it.

But how can we do that?

The procedure may be learned from that entity and as his Mercy and Grace, he has already taught us the same through *wahi*. To be in touch with *wahi* will give one the everlasting life. Yes, that life will be a good one if one has committed himself to *wahi*, positively; but if not, then that everlasting life will be a terrible one.

ii.   Intellect, as we said, is a sense and also a creature, and creatures are limited. So the approach of this sense is also limited, and there are things and issues beyond these boundaries, for which the human needs another source, and that is *wahi*.

iii. The Intellect is also affected like other senses, so this is not the certain ultimate source. That is why the *wahi* is needed.

iv.   The intellect cannot easily counter the culture and customs even if they are wrong. So humans need to have such a source, which can counter wrong culture and customs, and that is *wahi*.

v.   The intellect falls victim to superstitions where it is powerless. So humans need a source that can overcome the superstitions, and that is *wahi*.

vi.   The approach of intellect to certain things is different from person to person. This not only creates a lot of differences, but it can lead to turmoil, so there may be one agreed upon source, which may have no mistake, and that is *wahi*.

WHAT IS WAHI

Wahi means a hurried indication or *"pointing at in a hurry."* In the Holy Quran, this is used in different meanings, as follows:

i.   Indication:

"As Allah said that Zakariya [Zachariah] asked Allah: He said: "My Lord! Appoint for me a sign." He said: "Your sign is that you will not be able to speak to people for three nights with its days. Then he came out to his people from private worship place, and he told them by signs to glorify Allah Praises in the morning and in the afternoon." (19:10, 11)

This is elaborated in another verse:

"He said: "O my Lord! Appoint a sign for me. He said, your sign is that you will not be able to speak to people for three days [except by gestures]." (3:41)

ii.   Natural instinct and natural ability for natural function of a thing Allah said:

"And your Lord inspired the bees [put in their nature], saying: Take your habitations in the mountains and in the tree and what they erect. Then eat of all fruits and follow the ways of your Lord [that have been] made easy for you. There comes forth from their bellies a drink of varying color

wherein is healing for men, verily in this is, indeed, a sign for people who think." (16:68, 69)

"And he inspired in every heaven its affair." (41:12)

iii.   Bad Whispering:

Allah said:

"And so we have appointed for every Prophet enemies, devils from mankind and jinn [demons] inspiring one another with adorned speech as a delusion and deception." (6:112)

Also, He said:

"And certainly, the devils do inspire their friends to dispute [argue] with you." (6:121)

iv.   Good Inspiration:

Allah said:

"And We inspired the mother of Musa to suckle him, but when you fear for him then cast him into the river and fear not." (28:7)

In another verse, Allah said:

"And when I inspired the disciples [of Jesus] to believe in Me and My Messengers." (5:111)

Technically it means, Inspiration to a Messenger/Prophet by Allah.

WHY "WAHI" IS SENT TO

SELECTED PEOPLE?

Allah wanted humans to go towards Him in one united way. That is why He has chosen special people to receive *wahi* and commanded others to obey, follow and emulate them. If everyone had received *wahi*, there would never be any unity, unanimity and harmony. Also, as we said that intellectually even some people invent while others follow them. Therefore, some people are chosen and others will follow them.

Allah grows these people in a very natural and transparent way, and that is why most of these prophets are not grown under the eyes of their parents, and especially the fathers like *Ibrahim*. His father was an idol worshipper, but *Allah* developed *Ibrahim's* nature in a different way *Allah* said:

> "And indeed, We bestowed on Ibrahim his maturity / guidance aforetime, and We were well-acquainted with him." (21:51)

Prophet Moses was developed in the house of *Firaun* (Pharaoh), but under the eyes of Allah, as Allah said:

> "And that you may be brought up under My Eye." (20:39)

Also, He said:

"And have built you up for Myself (to convey My Message)."
(20:41)

Prophet Jesus (*Isa*) was born without a father, and he spoke when he was a newborn baby.

"He said, Verily, I am a slave of Allah. He has given me the Scripture and made me a Prophet. And He has made me blessed wherever I am and has enjoined on me prayer and charity as long as I live. And [to be] dutiful to my mother and made me not arrogant unblessed, and "Salam" [Peace be upon me the day I was born and the day I will die and the day I shall be raised alive." (19:30-34)

Also, Prophet Muhammad was born as an orphan, as Allah said:

"Did He not find you as an orphan and gave you shelter. And He found you illiterate so He guided you/guided through you." (93:6 and 7)

Allah made him in such a way that he presented himself to people if they have any objection to his character:

"Verily, I have stayed amongst you a lifetime [40 years] before this. Have you then no sense?" (10:16)

So nobody had any objection or even reservations about his noble character.

So the nature of a Messenger is clean and transparent enough to receive *wahi* as a common person cannot receive, bear and carry it. Their nature was transparent so sometimes they felt something with their common sense. But their feeling was such strong that they felt it as if they saw it with their eyes, as it happened to Moses when he was coming back to *Misr* from *Madian*, and he saw in the Holy Valley a light and said to his wife:

"Verily, I have seen a fire, perhaps I can bring you some burning brand from there or find some guidance at the fire." (20:10)

While it was not the same like fire one sees it with his eyes. Even their sleep does not break their *wudu* as the Prophet said:

My eyes get to sleep but my heart does not.

Moreover, their dream is a type of, and mostly it does not need any interpretation, and that is as certain as something they receive when awake and that is why Ibrahim took his dream literally and tried to sacrifice his son *Ismail (Ishmael)*:

"And when he (the son) was old enough to make effort/strive hard, he said: O my son! I have seen in a dream that I am slaughtering you. So look what you think! He said: O my father! Do that which you are commanded. If Allah wills you, you shall find me of the patient's Then when they had both submitted themselves and he had laid him prostrate on his forehead (on side of him), we called out to him: O Ibrahim! You have fulfilled the dream. Verily, thus we do reward the good doers. Verily, that indeed, was a manifest trial. And We ransomed him with a great sacrifice." (37:102-107)

Ismail grew up in *Makah*, not under the supervision of his father, but he showed him obedience, as Allah gave him a transparent nature. We can say that this is a position/status given by Allah. This is not a qualification, as Allah said:

"Allah knows well where he puts his Message." (6:124)

Also, He said:

"And they say why is not this Quran sent down to some great men of the two towns [Makah and Taif]. Is it they who will portion out the Mercy of your Lord?" (43:31,32)

HOW DID THE MESSENGERS

RECEIVE THE WAHI?

A Messenger and Prophet has to receive *wahi* as Allah:

> *"Likewise (the same way) Allah, the All-Mighty, the All-Wise sends revelation to you (O Muhammad) as (He sent revelation) to those before you." (42:3)*

Then the verses of *Surah An Nisa* gave the details:

> *"Verily, We have sent the revelation to you (O Muhammad) as We sent the revelation to Nuh [Noah] and the Prophets after him. We sent the revelation to Ibrahim [Abraham], Ismail [Ishmael], Ishaq [Isaac], Yaqub [Jacob], and Asbat (the offspring of the 12 sons of Jacob), 'Isa [Jesus], Ayub [Job], Younus [Jonah], Harun [Aaron] and Suleiman [Solomon] and to Daud [David], We gave the "Zabur" [Psalms]. And Messengers We have mentioned to you before, and*

> *"Messengers We have not mentioned to you, and to Musa [Moses], Allah spoke directly. Messengers are bearers of good news as well as of warning so that humanity should have no plea/excuse against Allah after the Messengers. And*

Allah is ever All-Powerful, the All-Wise. But Allah bears witness to that which He has sent down with his Knowledge [and leave], and the angels bear witness [as well], and Allah is All-Sufficient as a Witness." (4:163-166)

Also, Allah said:

"He has ordained for you the same Deen [faith] which he ordained for Nuh (Noah) and that which We have revealed to you (O Muhammad) and that which We ordained for Ibrahim [Abraham], Musa [Moses] and Isa [Jesus] saying: "You should establish [maintain, practice, implement] this Deen and make no division in it. Very hard for the polytheists is that to which you call them. Allah chooses for Himself whom He wills and guides unto Himself who turns [inclines] to him." (42:13)

Now it is clear that all the Prophets and Messengers used to receive Wahi, but how?

Allah said:

"It is not given to any human being that Allah will speak to him [face to face]. But by wahi *[inspiration] or from behind a veil, or that he sends a messenger (angel) to reveal what he [Allah] wills by his leave. Verily, he is Most High, Most Wise." (42:51)*

Here in this verse Allah has mentioned three ways of sending His Message:

(i)   Inspiration into the heart of the Messenger;

(ii)   Speaking to him from behind the veil, as he did to *Prophet Musa* (Moses) twice, and also to our Prophet Mohammed on the night of Ascension.

(iii) Sending him the archangel, *Jibril* (Gabriel). He used to bring Message to each and every Messenger and our Prophet as well. But how he did he come to our Prophet?

(a) Sometimes he used to inspire to him without being in an invisible shape as *Imam Ahmad* narrated from *Umar*:

"We used to hear a sound like buzzing of honey bees."

(b) Sometimes he came in the shape of a stranger, as *Umar said:*

"We were sitting with the Prophet when there appeared a strange man and when he left the Prophet asked us: 'Did you know who was this man asking me questions?' We said, "Allah and His Messenger know the best. The Prophet said: This was Jibril."

(c) Sometimes he came in the shape of a very handsome man, *Dih'yat Ul Kalabi*, and revealed himself to the Prophet.

(d) Twice he appeared in his own form, as Allah said:

"And indeed, he [Muhammad] saw him [Jibril] on the apparent horizon." (21:23)

Also, Allah said:

"The mighty in power [Jibril] has taught him [the Prophet]. [The one who is)] free from any defect [in body and mind], so he [Jibril] appeared clearly while he was on the high horizon. Then he neared and let down [became closer], and was at a distance of two bows' length or [even] nearer. So he revealed to His slave what He revealed. The heart [of the Prophet] lied not [made no mistake] in what he saw. Will you then even dispute with him about what he saw [meaning, Jibril that may be the Prophet has erred in his recognition – Nay.] And indeed, he saw him once again. Near a lote-tree of the utmost boundaries." (53:5-14)

The first appearance was in Makah, while the second time was upon the seven heavens. The *wahi* is of two types, as we mentioned above.

(1) *WAHI JALI* or *WAHI MATLU*

This is revealed from Allah. The recitation of its words is the best type of worship, as they are the speech and words of Allah.

(2) *WAHI KHAFI* or *WAHI GHAIR MATLU*:

The sense is revealed to the Prophet and he expressed the same in his words or through his actions and deeds. That is why Allah has ordered us to obey Him and to obey His Messenger as well. Allah has revealed the same in different context to make it crystal clear from every angle, so nobody may twist or misinterpret it so he said:

"Obey Allah and obey the Messenger" (4:59, 5:92, 24:54, 47:33, 64:12)

In these verses, he repeated the word *"Obey,"* which means that the obedience to the Prophet is as important as obedience to Allah. He said:

"And obey Allah and the Messenger." (3:32, 3:132)

Here in these verses he mentioned Himself and joined his Messenger to Himself in obedience by a conjunction, which means obedience means obedience to them both.

He said:

"And obey Allah and His Messenger." (8:1,20 and 58:13)

Here in these verses Allah attributed the Messenger to Himself, which means that the Messenger is His Messenger that is why his obedience is not negotiable.

Also, he said:

46

"And whosoever will obey Allah and His Messenger, will be admitted to gardens [in Paradise]." (4:13, 48:17)

"And whosoever obeys Allah and His Messenger, and fears Allah and keeps his duty to Him, such are successful." (24:52)

"And whosoever obey Allah and His Messenger, he has indeed achieved a great achievement." (34:71)

In these verses, Allah has mentioned the good result and reward of this obedience.

Also, He said:

"And whosoever obeys Allah and the Messenger, then they will be in the company of those on whom Allah has bestowed His Grace, of the Prophets, the people of Truth, the martyrs and the righteous. And how excellent these companions are." (4:69)

Even in one verse Allah said:

"And perform the prayer, pay the zakat (obligatory charity), and obey the Messenger." (24:56)

Which means you must obey and follow the Prophet about how to pray and pay.

Then Allah said:

"And We have sent you as a Messenger and Allah is enough as a Witness. One who obeys / will obey the Messenger, he has indeed, obeyed Allah, but one who turns away, then we have not sent you as a watcher/protector." (4:79,80)

Here in this verse Allah testified His Message followed by His obedience. This is what is meant by His Message is to be obeyed. Also, he applied the present and/or future tense when referring to the obedience of the Messenger. After that, He said that someone who obeys Allah is are not obligated to watch and protect someone who turns away from Him.

THE SUNNAH OF THE PROPHET

IS A SOURCE OF LAW LIKE THE

HOLY QURAN

Before we embark on this topic, it is important to know the difference between *hadith* and *sunnah*. The word *hadith* means *"a new thing."* It is the opposite of *qadeem*, which means *"old"* and *"ancient."* But technically *qadeem* is a term in *Ilm Ul Kalam* which deals with beliefs and its discussion. This quality is mentioned with regard to Allah and His attributes as well. It means everlasting since ever forever, and as the Holy Quran is the <u>Kalam</u> (word) of Allah and His attribute, so this is also *qadeem* like all His other attributes. And *hadith* (sometimes spelled *haadith*) literally means *"new,"* while technically it is said for the creature of Allah, which means that the whole world came into existence after that it was not.

The prophets of Allah are also humans, and also the creations of Allah. They are the chosen people and Prophet Muhammad, the last and final Prophet of Allah, is the utmost excellent personality. But he was a human and a creature as well. So he is also *haadith*. His qualities and attributes are *haadith*. His words are one of his qualities, so they are *hadith* also. The scholars have chosen this word to refer to his words, so *hadith* is the quality of every creature. *hadith* is used for the word of the Prophet or *haadith* is the quality of another creature and *hadith* is of words only. Sometimes Arabs use this for the words of others as well, so they might say, *"the hadith of Mr. So-and-so."* But when Muslims use the word, they are most often referring to the sayings and teachings of the Prophet, or the words of the Prophet as a derivative from a verse of Holy Quran.

Allah said:

And as for the favor of your Lord, you may relate (express). (93:11)

So His expression and the relation are derived from the word Hadith. And the Prophet made *dua* for those who preserve his teachings and relate the same, and he named them *muhadith, "one who relates hadith,"* so he said:

"O Allah! Be kind to those who relate Ahadith."

Then titling it as *hadith* as opposed to *qadeem* itself embodies that this *hadith* is the second source for the same subject as is the *qadeem*.

Sunnah is from *Sinn*, which means year, so *sunnah* means a practice of years or, in other words, an established practice or custom. It is frequently used for rule and law. Also, it is can mean "innovation" - good or bad, but the good one is appreciated, and the bad one is condemned.

The Prophet said:

"Whosoever established a good way in Islam, for him there is its reward and a reward equal to that of one who practiced it, and whosoever established in Islam a bad way for him there is its burden [sin] and a burden equal to that of one who practiced it."

The actions of *Sahabas* are also called *sunnah*, as the Prophet said:

"Indeed, whosoever will live after me, shall see much controversy so you may hold firmly my sunnah *and the* sunnah *of [my] righteous successors [the companions]."*

Now *hadith* stands for words and *sunnah* for actions, but they are used interchangeably, so we define them similarly and say that *hadith / sunnah* is the word, action, and sanction of the Prophet.

Sanction is the silent approval of the Prophet of the word or action of a Muslim when he saw someone saying or doing immoral, and he expressed his dislike for it, as the Prophet of Allah never kept quiet when he saw something against *Sharia*.

There are also some other terms commonly used in this field:

i.   *AL KHABAR*, which means *"news."*

As a special term it is employed in the meanings of stories of rulers, kings, nations, etc.; in other words, history. But scholars also used this word for *hadith* as the *Muhaddith* narrates *Hadith* and also the biography of the narrators and the stories in *ahadith* as well. But the one who narrates the stories of nations and rulers, etc., is called *muharrikh* (historian).

ii.   *AL ATHAR*, which literally means *"the footprints."*

It is used for any lasting effects or lingering vestiges, but specifically for sayings and actions of the *Sahaba* and the *Tabieen*. Some scholars said this term is for the sayings and actions of *Tabieen*, while the sayings and actions of the Sahaba are annexed to *hadith* and *sunnah* as we narrated a *hadith* in this regard where the Prophet said and the *sunnah* of the righteously guided successors. Then the word *athar* is also said for the *Hadith* and *Sunnah* of the Prophet and that is why *Imam Tahawi* has named his book *Shar'h Ma'aanil 'Aa'thaar (The Explanations and Meanings of Aathaar")* and that Book includes *hadith* and *Aa'thaar* as well.

Imam Tabrani named one of his books *Tahzeeb Ul Aathaar* and he put both *ahadith* and *Aathaar* in it. *Sunnah* is used for an old and ancient custom especially when it is a good one, and the ways of the Prophet, as he said:

"Knowledge is three: a muhkam verse, an established sunnah or a just fareedah and whatsoever is beyond that; that is an extra."

Here the Prophet is referring to the types of knowledge or the sources of knowledge. "*Muhkam verse*" means any verse of the Holy Quran. *"Established sunnah"* means the teaching of the Prophet, proven authentic via a known source. *"Just fareedah"* is any rule or issue derived from the Quran and *sunnah*. In *Ilm ul Kalam* or scientific beliefs, they say that *sunnah* is the teaching of the Prophet, of his companions, the *Tabieen*, and their followers as well, and also those concepts from authentic scholars, and the *ummah* passed down from generation to generation.

Near *Fuqaha* (scholars in Jurisprudence) *sunnah* is a practice that the Prophet used to do, but missed it only once or twice, so that is lower in status than *fard* and *wajib*, while the *Muhaditheen* said each and everything related from the Prophet: his words, action, sanctions, character, features, and whether it happened before he received the Message or after. Also the formation system of the creature, its functioning, and whatsoever Allah has adopted regarding his decrees in different time, which happened in the same way, is called the *sunnah* of Allah as Allah said:

"So no change will you find in Allah's sunnah *[way of dealing] and no aversion [to other] will you find in Allah's Sunnah." (35:43)*

All four of these terms are used to refer to the teachings of the Prophet. But to make a distinction the scholars say *Al Khabar Ul Marfoo* or *Al Athar Ul Marfoo* for the *hadith* of the Prophet while for that of a *Sahabi*, they say *Al Khabar Ul Mauqoof* or *Al Athar Ul Mauqoof*.

Also for the *hadith* of the Prophet they use the term *marfoo*. For that of a *Sahabi*, they say *mauqoof*, and for of a *Tabiee* they used the term *maqtoo*. If a *Sahabi* said such a thing that could not be known through the use of intellect and sense, (because all *Sahaba* were just, truthful, honest and trustworthy people who never lied), that type of his saying is called *hadith hukmi*. That is considered a *marfoo hadith*. So all these four terms are interchangeable, but when mentioned with its quality, such as like as if it is said *Al Khabar Ul Marfoo or Al Athar Ul Marfoo* then it means the *hadith* of the Prophet and if the quality mentioned is *mauqoof* then is saying of a Sahabi; if the quality mentioned is *maqtoo,* then it is the saying of a *Tabiee.*

HADITH IS A SOURCE OF LAW

As we said before, the Prophet received two types of *wahi* from the same source.

a. To believe in the Prophet means to believe in his words and actions and to have no doubt in any of his words or actions when that is proven through its sources and this is because:

a. His obedience is as important as obedience to Allah as we mentioned before.

b. Allah verified his words and actions:

"Your companion [the Prophet] neither went astray, nor he erred and he does not speak of desire. That is but a Wahi revelation revealed [to him]." (53:2-4)

Also, *Allah* said:

"And whatsoever the Messenger [of Allah] has given you [in the shape of his words, actions or sanctions] take it and whatsoever he forbids you, abstain [from it] and fear Allah. Indeed, Allah is severe in punishment." (59:7)

In this verse *Allah* used the word *ma*, a general term that includes every single word, action, and prohibition by the Prophet. Also, he said in the end and warned to *"fear Allah. He is severe in punishment"*, means if you will not do what he ordered then for sure you will be punished.

Also, *Allah* said:

"Those who follow [emulate] the Messenger, the Prophet who is illiterate the one they find written with them in Taurat *[Torah] and* Injeel *[Gospel] he orders them for good things and forbids them from evil things, he allows them the lawful things and prohibits them the filthy and dirty [unlawful things]." (7:157)*

This verse made it clear that he is a source for lawful and unlawful from Allah.

Allah also said:

"It is not for a believer, man or woman, when Allah and His Messenger has decreed a matter that they should have any option in their affair, and whosoever disobeys Allah and His Messenger, he has indeed strayed into a plain error." (23:36)

In another verse Allah said:

"But Nay, by your Lord, they cannot have faith until they make you (O Muhammad) judge in all disputes between them and find in themselves no resistance against your decision and accept (it) with full submission." (4:65)

As we know, the Messenger was a teacher, a trainer, a mentor and a role model as well. He used to teach two types of *wahi*; one is called *al-kitab* and the other one is called *al-hikmah*.

"And he [the Prophet] will teach them al-kitab *and* al-hikmah *"Al-Hikmah." (3:164)*

Al-kitab is the Holy Quran while *al-hikmah* is his teachings.

"Indeed in the Messenger of Allah you have a good model to follow for one who hopes (fears) Allah, the Last Day and remembers Allah a lot." (33:21)

A person who is considered a role model; he/she may not only be obeyed but must be emulated, as Allah said:

"Say (O Muhammad) if you [really] love Allah then emulate me, Allah will love you [make you the beloved of his angels, his true servants and for one another] and forgive your sins and Allah is Oft-Forgiving, Merciful." (3:31)

b. The Prophet was the first ever interpreter of the Holy Book through his words and actions, and whatever he said or did in this regard; it was revealed and inspired to him.

Allah said:

"This [the excellent] book, the verses thereof are perfected [filled with wisdom], then explained in details from one who is All-Wise, Well-Acquainted" (11:1)

In this verse, *Allah* said that all the verses of this book are full of wisdom and then explained. So the explanation thereof is also from *Allah* and for sure that is given to the Prophet.

Then what is that explanation and where is that?

There is no any other Quran given to the Prophet so far sure that is his words and actions.

Also He (*Allah*) said:

"And we sent down to you the zikr so you may explain clearly to people what is sent down to them so that they may think." (16:44)

Here in this verse Allah once said, *"We sent you the zikr"* and then he said to explain to them what is sent down to them. So what is sent down to them was the Holy Quran, which requires explanation, so the *zikr* is another revelation for the explanation described above, namely, is the *hadith* and *sunnah*.

Allah also said:

> "*Move not your tongue with it [the Holy Quran] making haste therewith. It is for Us to collect it [in your heart] and its recital [to give you the ability to recite or its first recitation by Jibril or its revision in every Ramadan]. So when We have recited it [to you] then follow up its recitation. Then it is to Us to explain it [to you]*" (75:16-19)

Here in these verses Allah mentioned the revelation and recitation and then the explanation that all these are to Us. So it means Allah sent the Book, the Prophet, and its explanation, and that explanation is the *hadith* and *sunnah*. Clearly, it is a must to believe in both types of *wahi* to practice by them both. Yes, the recital of the words of Quran is worship, and that is *ta'abbud* and these words are miracles as well. So no one can oppose it while that is not the case of *Hadith*. The Quran as a whole is *mutawatir* while *ahadith*, some of it is *mutawatir*, some are *mashhur* and some others are *aahad*. One who will reject a single verse of Quran will lose his *iman*, but one who refused a *hadith* due to the knowledge that is not a proven *hadith* may not be called a disbeliever. However, one who will reject *ahadith* as a source of *Sharia* will lose their *iman* for sure, as he rejected one type of *wahi* or even a significant portion of *wahi*.

Allah said:

> "*Verily, those who disbelieve in Allah and his Messengers and wish to make a distinction between Allah and His Messengers, saying we believe in some but reject others and wish to adopt a way in between, they are in truth disbelievers and we have prepared for disbelievers a humiliating torment. And those who believe in Allah and His Messengers and make no distinction between any of them, we shall give*

them their reward and Allah is ever Oft-Forgiving, Most Merciful." (4:150-152)

Now distinction between Allah and the Messengers means:

i.   To believe in Allah and not to believe in His Messengers, or

ii.   To believe in Allah and some of the Messengers and not to believe in some others, or

iii. To believe in the words of Allah and not to believe in the words of His Messengers.

So Allah Himself said they are disbelievers. In this regard, there are tens of verses. Also, there are hundreds of *ahadith* that make this concept clearer. However, as we are talking about *ahadith*, we have to talk about it by bringing proof and evidence, not from *ahadith*, but those sources that the opponents also believe in.

So besides the Holy Quran, another reliable source is the intellect. As we mentioned before, many things are apparent to intellectual people, and the intellectuals of a specific field may be trusted. This is life, and it is the practice as well. And the Prophet of Allah is the ultimate and utmost intellectual and wise. It is a known fact even to non-Muslim scholars as well. So whatever he said or practiced is logical, reasonable and beneficial. Yes, the only thing is that whether it is preserved as is or not. This is the ultimate objection the opponents have. So we will now proceed to discuss it.

Human Being, a Unique Creature:

a.   Allah, the Sole Creator of the entire universe, has created humanity as a unique type of creature, having salient features and exemplary qualities. He appointed him as his viceroy and agent on earth. This is a matter of great honor for the humanity. As an agent of Allah, he is given capability and talent to utilize his world and the things therein.

Allah said:

"And indeed, We have honored the children of Adam, and we carried them [given them the control] on land and sea. And We have provided them with pure lawful things. And We preferred them above many of those whom We have Created with a marked preference." (17:70)

Allah also said:

"Then We made you generation after generation after them so that we may see, how you do act." (10:114)

Like any other creation of Allah, humanity has been given their duties and they are given free will as well, because this is a test.

"And by human nature and its proportional perfection (abilities and capabilities), He inspired it with its evils and its piety." (91:7,8)

However, Allah also made a complaint from humanity, that all types of his creations fulfill their natural duties smoothly. Humanity who is blessed with intellect and legally bound constitutionally to perform their obligations and to obey the Commandments of Allah and the teachings of his messengers.

"Truly We have given amana [natural responsibilities] to the heavens [heavenly bodies as], to the earth and mountains, so they declined (not) to bear it and were afraid of it [rejection] and man left [as Imam Zajjaj said that 'Hamal' means leaving]. Indeed, he is unjust and ignorant." (34:77)

b. Humans have a particularly unique structure having all the requirements of animals, like food, drink, libido, shelter, and protection from any harmful things. However, as they have the element of intellect, so they have three extra characteristics regarding these requirements:

59

(i) Eagerness for intellectual approach and not only material objects.

(ii) Seeking purity and beauty and value so they try to have delicious food, fresh water, an attractive spouse and a beautiful, comfortable house.

(iii) Innovation and its adoption: The intellectual approach is different, though all of them try to find and make something more useful. Some of them succeed to innovate it and others who want the same, but they could not innovate it, they adopt the innovations of these others and follow them.

Now as human beings have two basic aspects:

1. PHYSICAL REQUIREMENTS:

They are looking for an intellectual approach and beauty and follow the intellectual approach of others regarding certain things they want but could not invent.

2. SPIRITUAL REQUIREMENTS:

In this field also they need satisfaction, mental peace, and tranquility, which they can have through religious practices the way ordered by Allah, their Sole Creator and Lord, and taught and shown practically by his messengers, who are the intellectual personalities and the guided people, receiving revelation and inspiration from Allah. So those who do not have the same approach and source must follow these messengers, like they follow the inventors of objects they use. This is logical and reasonable.

Allah wants humans to be close to Him.

How is it possible to be close to Allah?

Allah said:

> "O you who believe! Do your duty to Allah, fear Him and
> seek the means of approach to Him, and strive hard in His

Cause as much as you can, so that you may be successful."
(5:35)

It is a known fact that one can get closer to Allah through submission to Him; he will surrender to His Sovereignty and obedience of His Commandments. This submission and obedience must be in every aspect of human life. For this purpose, Allah sent books, scriptures and messengers to guide the humans towards the Will of Allah. These books are the source of laws. The sayings and practices of the messengers are the interpretation of these books and also another source of laws. Their actions and deeds are extra important.

When any inventor or manufacturer makes something that is useful and valuable, they send with it an instruction manual. If that machine and its production are extra valuable or complex, then the manufacturer will often send an engineer along as well. This person can demonstrate, teach, and guide others how to operate it properly.

Now this world, its utilization, human beings and their life to get success and prosperity in the Hereafter, is extra valuable. Allah not only sent books but messengers as well, to teach humanity how to behave. More than that, Allah has sent a majority of the Messengers and Prophets without giving them any book or scripture, as they received the Commandments of Allah through inspiration in their hearts and minds. Nevertheless, there is not a single example of Allah sending a book or scripture without a messenger. It means that a messenger can be without a book, but no book can be without a messenger, as he has to be the role model. That is why Allah made them in such a perfect way that they were given maturity and piety. The message and their life before the message are presented as an example.

Allah said regarding Prophet Ibrahim (as):

"And indeed, We bestowed aforetime on Ibrahim, rush'd [maturity and guidance]. And We were well aware of him. Now aforetime means "Before Message." (21:51)

Regarding Prophet Musa, Allah said:

"That you may be brought up under My Eye [supervision]."
(20:39)

"And have made you for Myself." (20:41)

Regarding Prophet Muhammad, Allah said that when the people of Makah objected to his Message and revelation:

"And when our clear verses are recited unto them [then] those who hope not for their Meeting with Us, say: "Bring us a Quran other than this or change it." Say: "It is not for me to change it on my accord. I only follow that which is revealed unto me. Verily, I fear if I were to disobey My Lord, the torment of the Great Day." Say: "If Allah had so willed I should not have recited it to you, nor would He have made it known to you. Verily, I have stayed amongst you a lifetime before that. Have you then no sense?" (10:15,16)

So Prophet Muhammad presented his forty years of life as proof of his honesty, that his personality was a role model even before the Message. That is why all famous messengers were brought up without the supervision of their parents. The father of Ibrahim was not only a disbeliever but also against *Ibrahim*, Musa was brought up in the house of *Firaun*, an archenemy of both Allah and Musa. Prophet Jesus had no father to guide and protect him. And *Prophet Muhammad* was an orphan. The purpose was to bring them up under the Eye of Allah to be a role model for their words and actions as well. Then Allah protected their words and actions for his followers, and especially those of *Prophet Muhammad*. Not only that but all those who related the same their history and biography are safe and protected as well.

Revelation and Protection:

Allah said:

"Verily, We, it is We, Who have sent down the zikr *[Revelation and inspiration] and surely We will guard it [from corruption and distortions]." (15:9)*

Prophets before our Holy Prophet received the Message. Some of them received it verbally while some others received it in written or inscribed form. Our Prophet received the same verbally through archangel Gabriel or was inspired by Allah. Then both types are protected and guarded by Allah as promised by Him.

"And We have never sent before you but men, whom We revealed to/inspired, so ask people of zikr *if you know not. [We sent them] with* bayyinat *and books, and We have sent down to you [O Muhammad!] the* zikr *in order to explain to the mankind what is sent down to them and that they may think/ponder upon. (16:43,44)*

In these verses it is made clear that:

1. *Wahi* (revelation and inspiration) was given to them and you as well.

2. This is an issue that is known to people of *zikr*, which are those who have expertise in this field, and they have intellectual approach therein, so everyone should not talk about it, but they may ask for this expertise.

3. They were provided books and *bayyinat* with clear rules and laws. Besides books as inscribed were given to a few of them, others were given inspired rules, which they expressed or practiced, and that became law.

4. You are given *zikr* to explain what is sent to them.

Here are two things:

a. *Zikr* certainly means something other than Quran as Quran is mentioned as *"what is sent down to them"*, and

b. That is to be explained by that *zikr*. Moreover, *zikr* is also given by Allah and that is the sayings and practices of the Holy Prophet.

5. So they may think about this very important issue that Holy Quran is in need of that *zikr* for its explanation.

Allah said:

"This is the Book the Ayat of which are filled up with Wisdom and then explained in detail from the side of (Allah) the Wise and the Well-Acquainted." (11:1)

In this Ayat there are two points:

a. The Ayat of this Book are full of Wisdom,

b. Then it is explained in detail from Allah. *Thumma*, which means *"then"* and not *wa* which means *"and,"* meaning that explanation given by Allah is somewhere else and later on. It is not in the Quran itself, but Allah also gave it to us. So surely that is given to the Prophet, so it should be called *hadith*.

Allah also said:

"Move not your tongue with it [Quran] to make haste with it. Verily, on Us is its collection [in your heart] and its recital [repetition] so when We [Gabriel] recite it then follow [with concentration] his recital, then on Us is its explanation." (75:16-19)

Allah has taken the responsibility of its explanation, and that is also with the same word *thumma* which means *"then,"* so that must be a separate and different thing, and that is *hadith*.

Regarding the sayings and practices of the Prophet, Allah said:

"By the star when it comes down, your fellow [Muhammad] has neither gone astray, nor he seduced. Nor does he speak

of [his] desire. It is but Inspiration that is inspired in these verses." (53:1)

Allah verified every single word and act of the Prophet and said, that all of his words and deeds are based on *wahi* (revelation and inspiration). Then Allah has commanded us in tens of verses to obey the Prophet as he said, *"obey Allah":*

"Obey Allah and obey the Messenger."

Here Allah has repeatedly mentioned the word *ateeoo*, which means *"obey."* However, in another place He did not repeat the word in his phrase.

"And obey Allah and the Messenger."

The first one underlines the obedience of the Prophet. As far as laws and rules are concerned, is as important as the obedience of Allah. The latter means that obedience to Allah and the Messenger is one and the same.

In another Ayat it is said:

"Verily, those who disbelieve in Allah and His Messengers and wish to make a distinction between Allah and His Messengers [by believing in Allah and His words and not believing in His messengers or in their words and actions] and say: "we believe in some [means Allah and His words], and reject others [the messengers and their words and actions] they wish to adopt a way in between. They are in truth disbelievers, and we have prepared for the disbelievers a Humiliating Torment. Moreover, those who believe in Allah and His messengers and make no distinction between them, We shall give them their rewards. And Allah is ever Oft-Forgiving, Most Merciful." (4:150-152)

Then regarding the Prophet there are two things:

a) *ITA 'AT*, which means *"obedience;"*

b) *IT-TIBA*, which means *"emulation."*

Obedience is related to His Orders and Commandments and emulation is related to his deeds and actions. Obedience also refers to is his orders and deeds, which are Sharia (Islamic rules) and they are mandatory. Emulation is related to his habitual acts and deeds, which are a matter of privilege and virtue.

Allah said:

> *"And whosoever obeys Allah and His Messenger, he has indeed, achieved a great achievement." (33:71)*

This is obedience while regarding emulation.

Allah said:

> *"Say [O Muhammad!] If you [really] love Allah then emulate me, Allah will love you and forgive you your sins. And Allah is Oft-Forgiving, Most Merciful." (3:31)*

In brief, it means that the Messenger of Allah is a role model and good example to follow, to obey and to emulate.

> *"Indeed, in the Messenger of Allah you have a good example [role model] for one who hopes in [fear] Allah and the Last Day and remembers Allah much." (33:21)*

Moreover, a role-model personality must be obeyed and emulated in word and spirit in every aspect of life. The *hadith* and *sunnah* of the Prophet are also *wahi* like that of *Holy Quran*. The only difference is that *Quran* is called *wahi jali* or *wahi matloo* which means that word and meanings, both are given by Allah, while *hadith* and *sunnah* is *wahi khafi* or *wahi ghair matloo,* which means that the meaning is inspired by *Allah* and words are that of the Prophet.

Allah said:

"And Allah has sent down for you the Book and Wisdom, and He taught you what you used not know. And the Bounty of Allah on you is very great." (4:113)

A majority of *ulama* (jurists) said that Wisdom in such like *Ayat* is the *Sunnah* and *Ahadith* of the Prophet.

Allah said:

"And who obeys the Messenger [of Allah], he indeed, has obeyed Allah. But one who turned away then We have not sent you as a watcher over them." (4:80)

1. *AHADITH* AND ORIENTALISTS:

In every intellectual field one has to put one's trust in those who:

i.   Possess comprehensive knowledge of the field concerned;

ii.   Have full sincerity with that field and devotion to it. If that is a field of *deen* and religion, then they must have:

iii. A firm belief therein, and

iv.   They must be just, integrated, practical, pious and God-fearing people.

One who is either a non-Muslim or prejudicial (zealous, partisan) towards that religion, one having Malafied intention, or an ignorant Muslim, or who is influenced by orientalists, non-Muslims, so-called scholars or much more affected and impressed by western materialistic developments and secular scientific approaches, which has convinced them. But, even mentally mesmerized them that when they are that much forward in this scientific field so their research and findings must be believed even in the field of our religion. This is a slave mentality.

Now these Orientalists said that *ahadith* were not written in the time of *Prophet Muhammad*, but in the second century, so they could not be trusted.

Even though some other orientalists admitted that *ahadith* are written in the time of the Prophet. But the compilation was under the supervision of *Caliph Umar* son of *Abdul Aziz*, a guided *Caliph*.

WRITING OF AHADITH IN THE

TIME OF THE PROPHET

There are two stages or steps regarding this writing:

- Prohibition of the writing of *ahadith*.

- Permission of the writing of *ahadith*.

1. Regarding Prohibition.

There is only one Hadith that is authentic and that is related by *Imam Muslim* regarding *Abu Saeed Al Khudry*

> *"Don't write from me, and whoever wrote from me except Quran, then he may erase it. In one relation it is added, relate from me, that is not a blame/sin, and whoever will attribute to me, lying, he is making his dwelling in fire (of Hell)."*

Unauthentic / weak *ahadith* are as follows:

a) *ABU HURAIRA* said

> *the Messenger of Allah came out to us, and we were writing ahadith, so he asked: "What are you writing"? We said, ahadith we heard of you." He said, "A Book other than the*

Book of Allah, you mean?" "People before you did not go astray but only with books they wrote with the Book of Allah. Abu Huraira said: "I asked, 'should we relate from you O the Messenger of Allah?' He said: "Yes relate from me that is of no blame/sin, but whoever will attribute to me falsely, he is making his place in the fire. (Ahmad related it, but its narration chain is weak.)

b) *ABU SAEED AL KHUDRY* says:

"I asked permission of the Messenger of Allah to write ahadith, but he did not allow me." (Tirmizi and Darimi both narrated it. However, the narration chain is weak).

c) *ZAID IBNI THABIT* says

That the Prophet of Allah prohibited his hadith to be written (weak). This prohibition is related from Abu Saeed-Al-Khudry, Ibni Masud Abu Musa-al Ash'ari, Abu Huraira, Ibni Abbas, Ibni 'Umar.

However, most of them disliked this writing and avoided relying upon it. They left to its memorization, and some later approved its writing, like *Abu Saeed Al Khudry, Ibni Masud, Abu Huraira* and *Ibni Abbas.* To them, the prohibition by the Prophet is either repealed or abrogated later on, or it was conditional, which means not to write it mixed with *Holy Quran.*

Now looking back into all these *ahadith* of prohibition, the only authentic *Hadith* is that of *Abu Saeed Al Khudry.* Later on he approved its writing, and this is a well-known rule that a Sahabi (when practice/act or give *fatwa* (juristic opinion) other than that he narrated before. Means that the narrated concept is abrogated, as the companion never intentionally violated a proven rule of *Sharia.*

2. Regarding permission of writing, there are a few *ahadith* and that number has approached the level of *mutawatir* (which could never be rejected) and these are as follows:

1. The Messenger of Allah when he delivered his sermon in Hajj, a companion from Yemen namely *Abu Shah* asked the Prophet if he could write the same for him.

The Prophet ordered:

"Write down [the sermon] for Abu-Shah." (Bukhari)

2. *ABDULLAH IBNI AM'R* said,

"I used to write everything I heard from the Messenger, and I wished to memorize it. The Quraish (some people of that tribe) prohibited me and said: 'You write everything from the Prophet you hear, and he is a human being, speaks in passion and anger.'" I mentioned this to the Prophet. He indicated with his finger towards his mouth (tongue) and said: "Write! I swear by one in whose hand is my soul [Allah] nothing comes out of it [mouth], but the Truth [right words].'" (Ahmad, Abu Dawud, and Darimi).

3. *ABU HURAIRA* says,

There was none from among the companions with ahadith more than I have but Abdullah Ibni Am'r, as he used to write and I was not. (Bukhari)

These *ahadith* are authentic, but there are less authentic ones.

One companion complained to the Prophet about the weakness of his memory.

The Prophet said to him:

"Seek the help of your right hand for memorization [i.e., write it down). (Tirmizi and Baihari).

Abdullah Ibni Am'r and *Anas Ibni Malik* both relate from the Prophet:

"Register [write] this knowledge with writing)" *(Jami Bayanil Ilm)*

Scholars have reservations about the provenance of these two. *Rafi Ibni Khadeej* and *Abdullah Ibni Am'r,* both said:

"The Prophet said, when he was asked about the registration of hadith, "Write it, that is not a blame/sin."

A few of the companions of the Prophet used to write and advised others to do the same. They are *Abu Bakr, 'Umar, Ali, Hasan, Ibni Abbas, Abu Saeed Al Khudry, Anas Ibni Malik, Abu Umama al Bahili.* It also includes *Muawiya, Mugheera Ibni Shoba, Aisha, Ibni Masud, Abu Huraira, Bara Ibni Aazib Asma Binti Umais, Subai 'a Al Aslamia* and many others as well.

i.   *Ibni Abdul Barr* in his *Jami* (name of the Book in *hadith*) related that *Ibni Am'r Ibni Umaiya ad Dzumari* related a *hadith* from *Abu Huraira, Abu Huraira* did not acknowledge it. *Ad Dzumari* said,

"Yes, I heard it from you." Abu Huraira said, "If I have related the same to you then certainly it would be written with me." He went into his room where there were many books of hadith, and he found it there.

ii. Also, one of his students, *Hammam Ibni Munnabih,* wrote a book called *Sahifa Hammam Ibni Munnabih,* which is a compilation of *Hadith* from *Abu Huraira.*

Then the scholars said that prohibition of *hadith* writing was at the beginning of Islam

a.   Not to combine them with the Quran;

b.   Not to depend on it and leave its memorization;

c.   Or this prohibition was only for those assigned to the registration of Quran so they should not write anything else. *Khateeb*

Baghdadi and *Hafir Ibnus Salah,* both well-known scholars, said that regarding this permission there is a consensus and Ijma' has taken place.

As we know that every word of the Prophet is called *hadith*, and every act of him is called *sunnah*, but they are considered synonymous. But these terms are used in more than that, as silent approval of the Prophet. These are also called *sunnah* or *hadith*. Therefore, any letter or document written by the Prophet is called *hadith* as well. It is a well-known fact that Prophet wrote certain things himself, such as letters to various rulers, kings and chiefs.

A. He wrote to:

    a. The King of Byzantium

    b. The King of Persia;

    c. The King of Egypt, *Juraij Ibni Matta* or *Binyamin* and carried by *Hatib Ibni Abu Balt'a;*

    d. The King of Abyssinia

    e. The King of Oman;

    f. The King of Himyar;

    g. The King of Bahrain;

    h. The King of Ghasasinah;

    i. The King of Yamamah;

B. Also, he wrote letters to certain tribes like:

    1. *Bani Harithah Ibni Amar;*

    2. The People of Dama in Oman;

    3. The chieftain of *Jazam* and *Khurza'a* (tribes);

4. His letter he sent with *Nahshal Ibni Malik* for his tribe;

5. His letter to the robbers in *Tihamah* granting them amnesty if they accepted Islam;

6. His letters to tribes of *Mehrah, Khaisamah, Banu Nahad, Jurm, Ushairah, Banu Harith, Uzd,* People of *Hajar* and Kings of Himyar;

7. And many others.

C. His letters to rulers, Judges, and collectors of *Zakat*:

   (1) In his letter to *Am'r Ibni Hazm* when he was sending him to Yemen, there were details of purification, prayer, booty, charity, compensation for injuries, et cetera;

   (2) His letter to *Ala Al Hadrami*, the Governor or Bahrain regarding details of Prayer and Zakat;

   (3) His letter to *Amir al Juhani,* a collector;

   (4) His letter to *Qabeesa Ibn ul Makhariq*, another collector;

D. Treaties, Pacts, Accords and Agreements written on the orders of Prophet:

   1. Madina's treaty with the Jews of Medina right after migration to Madina to give them equal rights as citizens;

   2. The agreement with the tribe of *Damurah*, that their lives and properties are protected, and they have to join Muslims to defend Madina. This was written in the first year after migration;

   3. The agreement with the tribe of *Ghitfan* in the battle of Allies in the 5th year;

   4. The Pact of *Hudaibiyah* between Muslims and the people of Makah in year 6th after *Hijra*;

5. The Pact of the Prophet with the ruler of *Dumat ul Jundal* in the 9th year;

6. An agreement of peace with the people of *Eilah* at the time of the battle of *Tabuk*;

7. An agreement with *Bariq* Tribe when they visited the Prophet;

8. An Accord with *Aslam* tribe of Mutual Co-operation against any invasion from outside;

9. An alliance treaty with the tribe of *Juhainah;*

10. The peace treaty with *Banu Habiba* tribe;

11. A Pact with *Banu Thaqeef* from Taif;

12. An Agreement with a tribe of *Banu Ghaffar;*

13. An Agreement sent to people of *Jarba* and *Azrah* when a delegation of them visited the Prophet in the 9th year;

14. His treaty with the Christians of Najran to protect them and they have to pay *"Jizyah"*, a tax paid to an Islamic state by non-Muslim citizens or subjects of that Islamic state.

E. Contracts, Declaration of general amnesty and giving land to certain people:

1. A pardon for *Suraqah Ibni Malik;*

2. His permission to *Azraq Ibni Umar* to stay in *Makah* and marry from the tribe of *Quraish*;

3. A document that was given to *Zaid Al Khair* giving him some land;

4. A verification letter regarding the ownership of *Zee Khawan*, their assets;

5. A document to *Tameem Ad Dari,* gifting him some land;

6. A document regarding gifting a piece of land to *Abbas as Sullami;*

7. A document to *Aqeel Ibni Karb* giving him some land with water fountains, trees, and date-palm trees;

8. A written document to *Ruqad Ibni Rabee'a* giving him a farm in Yemen;

9. A written promise to *Banu Qushair,* giving them some land;

10. A document to a delegation of *Abdu Qais* mentioning their rights and duties therein;

11. A document regarding protection of *Qailah Binti Makhrama* and her tribe;

12. A document giving some farms to *Bilal Ibn ul Harith al Muzani.*

F. Sermons and speeches are written by the order of the Prophet:

(1) In his farewell Hajj after his sermon, one Abu Shah asked for that sermon to be written for him. The Prophet ordered in this regard as narrated by *Bukhari* and *Muslim;*

(2) *Imam Ahmad* related that a *Hadith* was written by his order for *Utban Ibni Malik*

G. Liberation and Emancipation documents:

1. The emancipation of *Banu Damurah* tribe from slavery;

2. The emancipation of *Salman Al Farsi* from purchase from *Ibni Abdul Ash'hal;*

3. A written document by the Prophet's order for Aslam Abu Rafi regarding his liberation, written by *Muawiya* and witnessed by *Abu Bakr, Uthman* and *Ali.*

H. A written document showing the names of the missionaries and envoys of the Holy Prophet as mentioned by *Ibni Ishat.* They were sent to kings and rulers. Also, he added these letters to that document. This document was in the possession of *Yazid Ibni Habib al Misri.* He sent it to *Imam Zuhari,* and he verified its authenticity.

I. A document showing the names and number of Muslims at 1500, as narrated by *Bukhari.*

J. Documents registered the names of combatants regarding every battle, helping in the distribution of booty and the rights of the martyred. The Prophet had appointed an Inscriber for this purpose.

INSCRIBERS OF THE PROPHET

Most of the companions of the Prophet used to write, and the Prophet was eager for them to learn how to write. That is why, from the captives of Badr those who were writers, the Prophet put a condition for their release to teach ten people of Madina how to write. It means that the Immigrant Sahaba were writers, but people of Madina were farmers, and the Holy Prophet of Allah was eager to teach them how to write.

However, officially the Prophet had almost 60 inscribers, recording *wahi*, *zakat*, Transactions sales and purchases, contracts, letters, agreements, treaties, et cetera.

Then they had different assignments like:

a) Those who used to copy the Quran;

b) Those who were writing what the Prophet ordered them to write;

c) Letters to heads of states, et cetera;

d) Inscribers of covenants, agreements, and charity;

e) Correspondence with Arabs;

f) Inscribers of laws;

g) Writers of battles and booty documents;

h) Permanent Inscribers who accompanied the Prophet to write every urgent affair;

i) Those who were writing the contracts and transactions of public;

j) Writers on call (when they were needed).

SAHABAH (COMPANIONS)

WROTE BOOKS IN HADITH

Reading and writing have been important in Islam from day one, as the first *wahi* mentioned:

> *"Read, in the name of your Lord, who created [the whole world], [He] created humanity from a clot [hanging on the wall of the womb like a leech]. Read, and your Lord is the most generous/the Most Honored /the honor giver, who taught with the pen. He taught humanity what they knew not [before]." (96:1-5)*

In these verses:

a) The order *"Read"* is repeated because of its importance;

b) Read whatever you read, but it must be in the name of Allah, meaning it must be lawful and the good pleasure of Allah must be the first ever aim;

c) He is the Nurturer and reading is the best nourishment;

d) He is the Creator of the entire universe and all of humanity as well, and He knows that humanity is given the talent and ability to utilize the entire world,

e) The Nurturer is the Generous, Honored and Honor-Giver. The more you read and learn the more you will receive honor and be generous in providing that to others;

f) For knowledge, reading, and learning, et cetera, one has to know how to write;

g) Humanity can learn everything with the pen as this will carry on the knowledge of one generation to the other and, in the same way, every subsequent generation will learn more and more.

Based on these orders and instructions the Companions used to memorize and write everything they used to hear from the Messenger of Allah.

A few of them wrote books as follows:

a. *As Sahifa as Sadiqa* by *Abdullah Ibni Am'r Ibn Ul Aas*, where those are 1000 *Ahadith* therein;

b. The book of *Sa'd Ibni Ubadah*;

c. The book of *Mu'ad Ibni Jabal*;

d. The book of *Abu Rafi*;

e. The *Sahifa* of *Ali Ibni Abi Talib*;

f. The *Sahifa* of *Jabir Ibni Abd Ullah*.

It means that recording of *Ahadith* and its compilation was going on in the lifetime of the Prophet, but it was on an individual basis like that of the Holy Quran. Then the Holy Quran was compiled for the first time altogether under the supervision of the state in the time of *Abu Bakr* and then *Uthman*. It was the case that *Ahadith* were compiled on a state basis in the time of *Khalifa 'Umar Ibni Abdul Aziz*.

Another important point is that the first three *Khulafa, Abu Bakr, Umar* and *Uthman* gave due importance to the compilation of the Quran. A few

Huffaz (people who memorized) of Quran were martyred in the battle of *Banu Hanifa.* It took place in the reign of *Abu Bakr* and *Umar* was afraid of losing the Holy Quran. *Umar* asked *Abu Bakr* to compile it all together. In the time of *Uthman,* the *Huffaz* got involved in differences regarding different *qiraat* (dialects/accents) in the battlefield. So *Huzaifah Ibn ul Yaman* asked *Uthman* to write it down in an agreed upon *qiraat,* and he did so.

This means that the *ahadith* were memorized by a lot of *Sahaba.* They gave due importance to its memorization from generation to generation. That is why they were not afraid of its extinction even if the *Huffaz* were martyred in the same way. Regarding its dialects, there were no big differences, so these *Khulafa* never felt any urgent need of its compilation like that of the Quran. The compilation of the Quran was completed in the time of *Uthman* under the state and government's supervision. Moreover, now it was the number of *ahadith* compilation, but due to various fields of differences, disputes, battles and its settlement *Ali* could not find time to start with it. As we said, Sahaba used to compile the same on their own.

WRITING AND COMPILATION IN

THE TIME OF THE COMPANIONS

Even though a lot of Sahaba wrote in this regard, here we will mention a few of them:

1. The letter of *Abu Bakr* to *Anas Ibni Malik,* when he appointed him as governor of Bahrain. In that letter, he told him about mandatory charity, referring it to the Messenger of Allah as narrated by *Imam Bukhari.*

2. *Imam Ahmad* narrated from *Abu Uthman An Nahdi* that we were with *Utbah Ibni Farqad* when he was the governor of Bahrain. *Umar* wrote to him numerous things. One was that the Messenger of Allah said:

    One who wears worm-silk in this world he will not have anything of it in the Hereafter, but only like this and he indicated to his index finger and middle finger.

3. In the case of *Umar's* sword, a written document was found where there the *zakat* of cattle was written *(Al Kifaya).*

4. *Ibni Abdil Barr,* in his book <u>*Jami Bayanil Ilm*</u> narrated from *Abdullah Ibni Khunais,* said,

*He saw students near Bara Ibni A'adzib writing with a pen
made of cane.*

5. *Anas Ibni Malik* used to dictate the *ahadith* to his students. However, when the students increased, he brought a register from his books. He put it in front of them and said,

   *"these are ahadith, I have taken from the Messenger of Allah
   I wrote it, and I got it verified" (Al Khateeb Al Baghdadi).*

6. *Ma'n* said that a book was brought out to *Abdur Rahman Ibni Abdullah Ibni Masud,* and swore that it was the writing of his father.

7. *Muawiya Ibni Abi Sufyan* asked *Mugheera Ibni Shoba* in a letter to write to him something he heard from the Messenger.

   He wrote that the Messenger prohibited (to say without inquiry) it is said, or somebody said, and for a lot of questions (or begging as profession), and to waste one's property. (Bukhari)

8. *Ahmad* related that *Ali* had a very famous Register where there were rules for injuries, compensation, blood money and emancipation.

9. *Imam Muslim* related that Ibni Abbas used to write the *ahadith* from Salma, the wife of Abu Rafi. The servant of the Holy Prophet said,

   "Ibni Abbas used to come to my husband with some wooden boards in his hand to write the Ahadith upon them."

10. *Samura Ibni Jundab* had a significant volume of *ahadith*, his son *Suleiman* and *Hasan Al Basri* related from that place as *Ibni Sa'd* related in *Tabqat.*

11. Sa'd Ibni Ubaidah compiled a book; his son used to relate from that book *(Shafi in Kitab Ul Umm).*

12. *Imam Ahmad* and *Ibni Hisham* narrated that *Mu'aadz Ibni Jabal* had compiled a book that came into the possession of *Ibni A'aidz,* and another book that came to *Musa Ibni Talha.*

13. *Ibni Abdul Barr* in *Jami Bayan ul Ilm* narrated from *Am'r Ibni Umaiya Ad Dumari* that he related a *hadith* from *Abu Huraira,* which he could not acknowledge. *Am'r* said,

   "I have taken this from you." Abu Huraira said, 'If it is so, then it must be written with me.' So he got a hold of my hand and took me inside his room where there were a lot of books, so he found that Hadith in there."

14. *Abu Rafi* had a book, where there was the *ahadith* of *Salamah* to *Abu Bakr Ibni Abdur Rahman (Al-Kifaya).*

15. *Hammam Ibni Munnabih,* one of the students of Abu Huraira, has written his *Sahifa* from *Abu Huraira,* Also, his other students like *Saeed Al Maqburi* and *Ibni Seereen* also wrote from the books of *Abu Huraira*

16. *Abdur Razaq,* in his *Musannaf,* said he acquired from the *Sahifa* of *Jabir Ibni Abdullah.*

17. In *Al Isabah,* it is written that *Shimoon Al Uzdi* had several books of *ahadith.*

18. *Rafi Ibni Khadij* had a collection *Ka'b Ibni Am'r* had a compilation of *ahadith*, and *Ibni Umar* had a few books.

19. *Hasan Ibni Ali* used to order his sons and nephews to write as it is *(Ibni Abdul Barr).*

These are a few examples of how *Sahaba* used to write and compile *ahadith.*

WRITING BY TABIEEN

Tabieen are the students of the companions of the Prophet. They used to write and compile *ahadith*. They are the people to whom the Prophet gave verification. He said,

> *"The best people are the people of my time, and then those of the successive generation, then their subsequent generation."*

According to *ulama* (scholars), people of the time of the Prophet are his companions, then the succeeding generation are known as *Tabieen* (students of the companions), then the next following generation are *atba ut tabieen* (students of *Tabieen*), but some other *ulama* said that the time of the Prophet is his lifetime, and then the following time are *Sahaba* (companions) and the next people are *Tabieen*.

So, *Tabieen* are authentic people in general based on this *hadith* and both the interpretation of this *hadith*. After their time there must be some standard criterion to find out who is authentic and who is not. So Tabieen were also writing and compiling the *hadith*.

A well-known *muhaddith* (scholar of *ahadith*) Saeed Ibni Jubair, who passed away in the year 95 after *Hijra* (migration of the Prophet to Medina), has written several volumes of *ahadith*. He used to travel with his teachers from the Companions, *Ibni Umar,* and *Ibni Abbas,* and to write from them even when he was riding on his camel. (*Ad Darimi* and *Ibni Abdul Barr*).

Khateeb Baghdadi in his book <u>*Tareekhi Baghdad*</u> (*A History of Baghdad*) mentioned that *Shahr Ibni Haushab,* who died in the year 100

(A.H.) had a compiled book of *hadith*. He used to dictate to his student from that book.

- *HIBBAN IBNI JUZ AL ASLAMI,*

Who died in the year 100, A.H. had a written collection of *hadith* (*Al Jarh Wat Tadeel,* 103 A.H.).

- *KHALID IBNI MI'DAN*

Had a big register of *ahadith* (*Tazkirat ul Huffaz*)

- *ABU QILABAH (104 A.H.)*

Had a significant collection, half of a camel load, which later on came to *Ayub* as *Sukhtayani* (*Tazkirat ul Huffaz and Al-Kifaya*).

- *HASAN BASRI (110 A.H.)*

Had a big book. He collected *ahadith* in it. Also he had a *tafseer* for the Holy Quran, a collection of his lectures, a collection of various issues, a book in the name of *Kitab Ul Ikhlas* and he used to dictate for his students from his collections (*Tabqat, Al Kifaya, Tazkirat ul Huffaz*).

- *ALI IBNI ZAID AL HANI (110 A.H.)*

Had a collection of *ahadith* in a few books, some of that came later on in the hand of *Ubaid Ullah Ibni Zahar* (*Tahzeeb Ut Tahzeeb*).

- *QASIM IBNI ABDUR RAHMAN AL SHAMI (112 A.H.)*

Had a prominent collection of *Ahadith*, which came to his student *Ali Ibni Yazid* (*Tahzeeb*).

- *ABDULLAH IBNI BURAIDAH AL ASLAMI (115 A.H.)*

Collected his A*hadith* therein, and *Matar Ibni Tuhman* benefited from it.

- *SULEIMAN IBNI MUSA AL ASADI (115 A.H.)*

Had a collection of *ahadith* (<u>*Meezan ul I'tidal*</u>).

- *TALHA IBNI NAFI (117 A.H.)*

Had a book, having 100 *ahadith* therein and *Imam Aamash* copied from them as *Talha* copied from the book of Jabir *(<u>Meezan</u>)*.

- *ATA IBNI ABI RABAH (117 A.H.)*

Is known for his writing and dictating it to his students. He wrote a book in *hadith* that he passed on to his son *Yaqub*. Also, he had *ahadith* written from *Ali* (<u>*Tahzeeb, Muqaddimat ul Jarhi Wat Tadeel*</u>).

- *MUHAMMAD IBNI SHAHAB AZ ZUHARI (124 A.H.)*

Is the famous scholar who wrote a lot of books in *hadith*, and also compiled books when he was officially asked to do the same by *Amir ul Momeneen Umar Ibni Abdul Aziz*. He has books on *hadith*, wars, and lineages. He used to put every *hadith* he learned on record, and the Sayings of *Sahaba* and *Tabieen* as well. He ordered his students not to attend any class without pen and paper *(<u>Al Jarh Wat Tadeel, Tazkirat ul Huffaz,</u> <u>Muslim, Tahzeeb</u>)*.

- *KHALID IBNI ABI IMRAN AT TUNISI (125 A.H.)*

Had a collection of *ahadith* that he wrote from *Tabieen* in Madina. He took it to Africa and related them there. *Sahnun Ibni Saeed*, in his book in *Maliki Fiqh*, and other scholars in Africa, relied on it (<u>*Tahzeeb, Al Jarh-Wat Tadeel*</u>).

- *YAZID IBNI ABI HABIB AL MISRI (128 A.H.)*

Had a collection in *ahadith* he wrote from *Ata Ibni Abi Rabah* and *Imam Zuhari*. The people of Egypt and others used to relate them *(<u>Tahzeeb</u>)*.

- ## *BAKR IBNI WASIL (130 A.H.)*

Had a book of *ahadith*. He died before his father so that book was given to his father *(Tahzeeb, Al Kifaya)*.

- ## *MUHADDITH HAMMAM IBNI MUNNABIH*

A well-known *Muhaddith who* had a book from his teacher *Abu Huraira* in the name of *Sahifa*. Later on the compilers of *ahadith* benefited from it, as *Sheikh Abdur Razzaq* put it in his *Musannaf,* and *Imam Ahmad* put it in his *Musanah*. Later on, *Dr. Hameed Ullah* got it from Syria and printed it. This original book is a good example of the earliest *hadith* writing *(Tazkirah, Sahifa, Musnadi Ahmad, Al Kifaya)*.

- ## *ALI IBNI ABDUR RAHMAN (139 A.H.)*

Had a book in *hadith*. He was very strict for his students to inscribe it as a whole *(Al Ma'arif, Al-Kifaya)*.

- ## *HUMAID AT TAWEEL (142 A.H.)*

Had a book in *hadith*. He copied it from the books of *Hasan Al Basri* and *Ekrama,* the student of *Ibni Abbas* (*Tahzeeb, Tabqat, Al-Ma'arif,* and *Taqeed ul Elm*).

- ## *HISHAM IBNI URWAH (146 A.H.)*

Wrote *ahadith*. He used to dictate to his students who were compiling his *ahadith*. Then they presented them to *Khalid Ibn ul Harith* and *Nuh Ibni Abi Mariam*).

These are only a few examples of compilation in that time; there are many more.

OFFICIAL COMPILATION OF

AHADITH

In the very beginning, this idea was brought up at the time of *Umar Ibn Ul Khattab*, but after that he thought this for almost one month, and later on he dropped it, because:

i.   Sahaba relied on memorization more than writing;

ii.   Sahaba were of the view that if official compilation takes place, people will leave their individual efforts of compilation and memorization;

iii. The first three *Khulafa – I - Rashideen* (Righteous Successors) *Abu Bakr, Umar* and *Uthman* gave due importance to the compilation of Holy Quran, until it was completed in the time of *Uthman*, whereas during the time of *Ali* and *Muawiya* was very much engaged in conflicts, and rulers after *Muawiya* were not enthusiastic about religious services until *Abdul Aziz Ibni Marwan* (85 A.H.), the governor of Egypt. He wrote to *Kathir Ibni Murrah Al Hadrami* to write the *ahadith* he learned from *Sahaba*, except *Abu Huraira,* because his *ahadith* were already written *(Tabqat, Tahzeeh).*

iv.   *Kathir Ibni Murrah* met with 70 Sahaba from those participated in *Badr,* in *Himas* (Syria). It means that the idea of an official compilation of *ahadith* was practiced in the time of *Amir Abdul Aziz Ibni Marwan,* and then his son Umar Ibni Abdul Aziz ordered its official compilation. He wrote to his governors in different provinces:

"Look for the Hadith of the Messenger of Allah and collect it." (Fath Ul Bari).

Moreover, he wrote to the people of Medina:

"Look for the Hadith of the Messenger of Allah as I am Afraid that [this] knowledge will efface, and its scholars will Vanish." (Sunan ad Darimi).

Also, he wrote to his governor *Abu Bakr Ibni Amar Ibni Hazm:*

"Write (and send) to me [all] that with you from the Hadith of the Messenger of Allah and the Hadith of [Lady] Amrah [the daughter of Abdur Rahman Ibni Abi Bakr, the niece of Aisha and the maternal aunt of Abu Bakr Ibni Hazm. She had memorized all ahadith of Aisha], as I am afraid that knowledge and knowledgeable people will vanish [and we will lose it] (Bukhari and Darimi).

Ibni Hajar reported that he wrote:

"That I am afraid that knowledge and its scholars will vanish, and do not accept [anything else] but the Hadith of the Holy Messenger of Allah, and the scholars must spread and divulge the knowledge so those who do not have it, they may have it because knowledge does not vanish until it is kept secret [confined]." (Fath ul Bari).

In the same way he wrote to various parts of the country:

"Give orders to knowledgeable people to spread out into their mosques because [spreading] Sunnah [hadith] is forgotten."

Imam Darimi quoted that he wrote:

> *"There is no room for anyone to give his opinion in the Book of Allah, but opinion could be given regarding the issue where there is nothing in the Book of Allah nor the Sunnah of the Messenger of Allah. There is no room for an opinion against the Sunnah of the Messenger of Allah."* *(Darini)*

So, he ordered *Muhammad Ibni Shahab Al Zuhari* and others to collect the Sunnah *(Jami Bayanil-Elm)*. *Abdullah Ibni Zakwan* relates that he saw *Umar Ibni Abdul Aziz* gathering the scholars. They brought him *ahadith* in abundance. He used to discuss and debate the same with them to find out the correct one. As we said already that *Abu Bakr Ibni Hazm* wrote *Ahadith* for *Umar* what he ordered him to do. However, *Imam Zuhari* did compilation as a whole. That is why he said that no one compiled these *ahadith* before him *(Irshad us Sari, Todreeb ur Rawi Al Jarh Wat Tadeel)*. Then he sent the copies of that compilation to every part in the country. *(Jami Bayanil Elm)*

COMPILATION AFTER TABIEEN

All this compiling started in the first half of the second century, and it went on until all was compiled in the best way in the third century, and that was the golden time for compilation. Certain *ulama* compiled *ajza*, which is the plural of *juzz* which means that they compiled *ahadith* relating a particular issue and subject. For example, *Imam Shabi* compiled a *juzz* for divorce *(Hadi us Sari)*. Also, these scholars did not only compile *hadith* of the Prophet but also the sayings of the *Sahaba* and their students as well as their juristic opinions.

These scholars are listed below, with their death dates:

- *ABDUL MALIK IBNI ABDUL AZIZ IBNI JURAIJ* (150 A.H.) at Makah;

- *MUHAMMAD IBNI ISHAQ* (151 A.H.) at *Medina;*

- *MA'MAR IBNI RASHID* (153 A.H.) at *Yemen*;

- *SAEED IBNI ABI AROOBA* (156 A.H.) at *Basrah*;

- *ABDUR RAHMAN IBNI AMAR AL AUZAEE* (156 A.H.) at Syria;

- *MUHAMMAD IBNI ABDUR RAHMAN IBNI ABI ZIB* (158 A.H.) at *Madina*;

- *RUBAY'YI IBNI SUBAIH* (160 A.H.) at *Basrah*;

- *SHOBA IBN UL HAJJAJ* (160 A.H.) at *Basrah*;

- *SUFYAN IBNI SAEED ATH THAWRI* (161 A.H.) at *Kufa*;

- *LAITH IBNI SA'D* (175 A.H.) at *Egypt*;

- *HAMMAD IBNI SALAMA IBNI DEENAR* (176 A.H.) at *Basrah*;

- *MALIK IBNI ANAS* (179 A.H.) at *Medina*;

- *ABDULLAH IBN UL MUBARAK* (181 A.H.) at *Khurasan*;

- *HUSHAIM IBNI BASHIR* (188 A.H.) at *Wasit*;

- *JARIR IBNI ABDUL HAMID AD DHABBI* (188 A.H.) at *Ra'y*;

- *ABDULLAH IBNI WAHAB* (197 A.H.) at *Egypt*;

- *SUFYAN IBNI OYAINAH* (198 A.H.) at *Makah*;

- *ABDUR RAZAQ IBN UL HAMMAN AS SAN'ANI* (211 A.H.) at *Yemen*.

Their compilations carry the titles as *Musannaf, Sunan, Mu'atta, Jami, Musnad,* et cetera. Based on these facts it became clear that the enemies of Islam were confusing this subject. They say that writings and compilation of *ahadith* took place in the second century, which is wrong, as writing and compilation of *ahadith* were going on at the time of the Holy Prophet even. The official compilation took place in the time of *Umar Ibni Abdul Aziz*.

IMPORTANCE OF ILM UL

HADITH

Ilmul Hadith is an essential science as it is the second source of Islamic Sharia, and it is an interpretation of the Book of Allah by the Messenger of Allah. However, it is also a very difficult science as it is based upon narration, and for narration it is necessary to know who narrated what is being written.

To this end, we must know about the narrators' lives, their characters, their piety, their memory, their commitment and devotion to their faith. And we must find out how they were regarded by other scholars of this field and science.

It is a type of miracle that his followers properly preserve the Prophet's *ahadith*. They number over seven hundred thousand, along with the biography of all its narrators who are almost five hundred thousand, as Dr. Springer said, *"Is preserved as well."* In this book, we will try our best to give a brief explanation of *Usool Ul Hadith,* which means the rules and the types of *ahadith*. Many people quote someone and say it is a *hadith* even though it is not. Although there are people who bluntly and abruptly say regarding a *hadith*, that it is *zaeef* even though he does not know the definition of a *saheeh* or *zaeef hadith*. By saying it is *zaeef* he is trying to throw away the *hadith*. If a *hadith* is *zaeef,* that is only an academic issue, and that is an issue of research and *ijtihad*. That is why the scholars differ from each other in this categorization. After being *zaeef*, it could still be elevated to the level of a *maqbool hadith* and would be made a base for a *sharee* issue.

Additionally some people think that *ahadith* or *Saheeh ahadith* are only in the book of *Imam Bukhari* or the book of *Imam Muslim.* The forget that *Bukhari* and *Muslim* themselves said we could not compile all *Saheeh ahadith* but only a group of them. It is worth mentioning that all of the *ahadith* of *Imam Bukhari* and *Muslim* are *Saheeh.* It is due to the requirements they mentioned, which is another issue that the *hadith* itself is *Saheeh.*

Here we have tried to make it as simple as we can. However, this science is such a science that the students of Quran and Sunnah study it at the masters or Ph.D. level because it is not very easy to understand. We will make a *dua* that Allah make it easy for us to understand, make it a source of knowledge and guidance for all, and may Allah accept it from us and all those who benefit here. Ameen.

This science is very technical and difficult to understand. Certain topics are even more difficult, which is why we have not included them in this book. However, we have included them in our Arabic book of <u>Usool Ul Hadith</u> in detail. May Allah accept these efforts.

USOOL UL HADITH

Usool is the plural of *asl,* which means *"root"* or *"base,"* but it is also used to mean *"rules."* In this book, we mean what are the rules for *ahadith* and its categorization, which is called the science of *hadith.*

Wahi, or revelation, is of two types:

1. *WAHI JALI*:

Where the words and source both are revealed from Allah.

2. *WAHI KHAFI*:

Where the source is revealed or inspired, and the words are that of the Prophet of Allah.

Wahi is needed logically as human senses and intellect are the two physical means and sources of knowledge, and they:

1. Have a limited capacity;

2. Can be manipulated or deceived;

3. Can only sense physical and material things;

4. Cannot counter superstitions and customs.

5. Moreover, no one's intellect can be considered a perfect and final one. Nor will people agree upon that while these are things, realities, and facts beyond that. Moreover, the spiritual want to

know how to connect to Allah and how to achieve tranquility through connection with Him.

This must be asked from Allah himself and Allah through His Mercy already sent us the *wahi*, so *wahi* is needed.

Wahi jali is Quran and that is *mutawatir*, which means it is taken from the Prophet by more than one hundred thousand Companions. *Wahi khafi* or *Hadith* and *Sunnah* have also been taken from the Prophet by his companions (the *Sahaba*). Some of them are considered *mutawatir* while others are not, and that is why the science of *Hadith* is difficult but also important. It is important as it is *wahi* and the source of *deen* and *Sharia*, and it is challenging as to know the status of any specific *hadith*.

As a preface, we will say that the Prophets and Messengers had been receiving *wahi* from Allah sometimes in written form, sometimes verbally, and sometimes through inspiration. Our Prophet received the Holy Quran verbally both its words and sense. He received *hadith* through inspiration, but only its sense, and later on he expressed the same sense in his words or practice, and the Sahaba preserved it and practiced it as well. This is why, for a *hadith*, the *ummah* looks at the practice of Sahaba and then they find out the status of that *hadith* there from.

As a whole, the Quran is *mutawatir*, which means innumerable people passed it down from generation to generation. Therefore, it does not require any narration chain or authentication. There is no need to determine who acquired it from whom, or their status and position. Among *ahadith* there are *mutawatir hadith* and there are non-*mutawatir hadith*, and the latter are of two types, either *mashhur*, or *aahad*. The subject mentioned therein is *mutawatir* as it is in a great number of *ahadith*. Alternatively, some are *mutawatir amali*, meaning the subject has been taken into consideration and practice by innumerable Sahaba. However, these later two types are the subject of the *Fuqaha* (jurists), while we are focusing on the science of *hadith*. Our subject is the first type of *mutawatir*, which has been narrated by many narrators.

This science is an important topic in *deen* but it is very complex. That is why so many people who could not understand this subject or do not have time to study it in its proper way try to get rid of it by saying,

> "The Holy Quran is more than enough as a source of Sharia,"

Or they question the authenticity of *hadith*. They do not understand that this type of thinking or talking could put the *iman* at risk. If someone wants to study our book, they can study *The Authenticity of Hadith*, which will be good for them, *Insha'Allah*.

Usool Ul Hadith is an essential and critical part of *ilm ul hadith* or the science of *hadith*. *Hadith* is an Arabic term that is the opposite of *qadeem*. *Qadeem* means *"ancient,"* and *hadith* means *"new."* Allah is a *qadeem* entity who exists because of Himself and He is eternal so His attributes and qualities are *qadeem*. Since *kalam*, or *"word and speech"* are one of His attributes, these are *qadeem*, and the *Holy Quran* is His word, so it is also *qadeem*. The words of His Messenger are called *hadith*. The *hadith* is mostly used for his words while his deeds and actions are called *sunnah*. However, later on these two are used interchangeably, and even his sanctions are called *Hadith* or Sunnah as well. Also, the *athar*, Proverbs, and actions of the Sahaba are called *hadith*.

Regarding the *Sunnah*, however,

The Prophet himself said,

> "So you must keep to my sunnah and the sunnah of the rightly guided successors of mine [the Sahaba]." (Narrated by Abu Dawud and Tirmidhi)

HADITH AND SUNNAH HAVE

TWO PARTS:

i)   A *sanad* or the narration chain through which it is narrated;

ii)   A *matan* or the very text of it.

The *muhaditheen* have discussed these both thoroughly. First, they spoke about the narrators individually to determine they are trustworthy people. Second, they talked about the continuity of the chain and for the purpose mentioned above they researched the lives of all these narrators. Third they articulated about the very text of the *hadith*. Based on these details they then classified the *ahadith* of the Prophet.

This is a specific science for this expertise and those who study it are called critics, and they are considered as the authority in this regard. This study is based on their research, this is why sometimes the critics have a difference of opinions regarding a narrator or about a specific *hadith*.

Before proceeding further towards our subject, we would like to mention that certain words mentioned here in this subject are terms, and they may not be taken into consideration in its specific literal meaning only. For example, the term *saheeh* literally means *"correct"* but here as a term that is a type of *hadith* with specific qualities. As another example, the term *zaeef* means *"weak."* However, here it means a *hadith* that lacks a specific quality or qualities, but this does not mean that it is not a *hadith*. In other words, we can say that a healthy person is a human, and an ill one is a human as well. A *hadith* could be *zaeef* based upon the research of one critic but to another, it might be *saheeh*. Sometimes a *hadith* could be *zaeef* based on one narration chain but the based on another one it could be *saheeh*. Alternatively, a *hadith* could be *zaeef* based on every narration chain, but when all put together, they raise it to the upper level. Or a *hadith* could even be *zaeef* as far as its very wording is concerned but not in its meaning. As the same meaning is mentioned there with a different wording in a *saheeh hadith* or the *hadith* is a *zaeef hadith* but the subject was the practice of Sahaba. In this situation, the first two points are related to this topic while the latter two are related to *Fiqh* and *Fuqaha*.

Narration is either from the Prophet, which is called *marfoo*, or from a Sahabi, which is called *mauqoof* or *athar*. It must be from a Tabiee as *maqtoo* and also *athar*, or the story of Kings and Nations, which is called *khabar* or history. However, if a Sahabi said such a thing, which could never be known through reason and intellect, then for sure he heard it from the Prophet. So it is to be considered a saying of the Prophet because none of them has ever told a lie. Something that is narrated from the Prophet or about him will either be his words, which are called *hadith*, or his actions, which are called Sunnah. If he or he saw someone saying or doing something and he did not disapprove of it or stop him, that is his silent approval or sanction, and this is also considered *hadith* and Sunnah. If that is something about any form of his feature or functions, then that is called *as seerah* or *ash shamaail*.

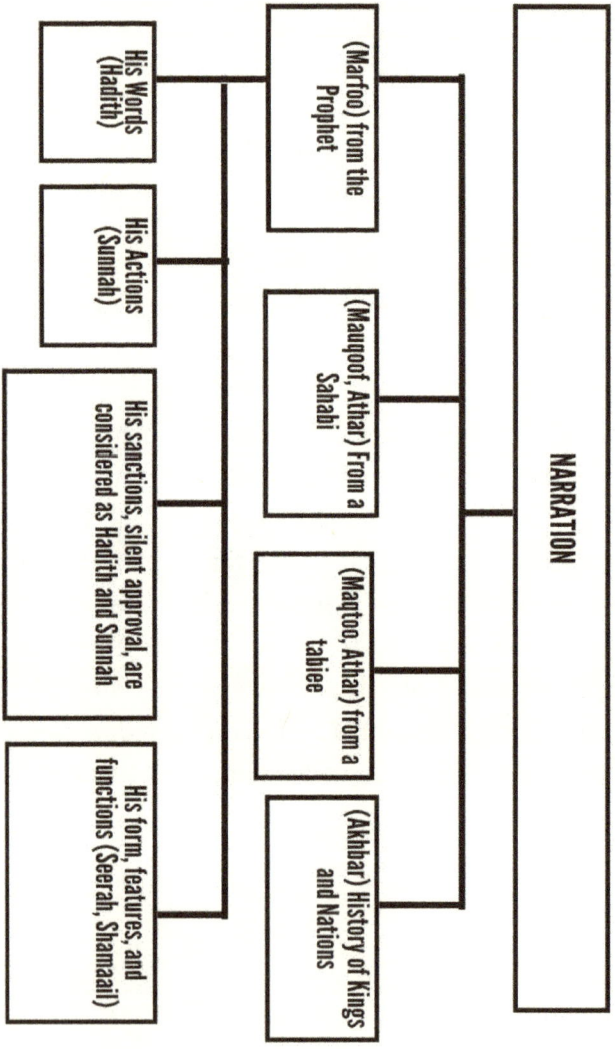

NARRATION

- (Marfoo) from the Prophet
  - His Words (Hadith)
  - His Actions (Sunnah)
  - His sanctions, silent approval, are considered as Hadith and Sunnah
- (Mauqoof, Athar) From a Sahabi
- (Maqtoo, Athar) from a tabiee
- (Akhbar) History of Kings and Nations
  - His form, features, and functions (Seerah, Shamaail)

Then if a *Hadith* is transmitted by a limited number of narrators, then that is *Al Khabar Ul Wahid*. If many narrators transmit it, then it is called *Al Khabar Ul Mutawatir*.

Al Khabar Ul Wahid is either:

1. *Al Ghareeb* or *Al Fard* if there is only one narrator.

Ghareeb is the first step. Next is if more than one *Sahabi* narrates it, and there is another type of *Ghareeb*: if, in the first step, more than one *Sahabi* narrated it, but in later generations and steps, there was only one narrator who did so.

2. *Al Azeez* are *hadith* that are narrated by two narrators in each step.

When the chain of narration and the text of these two types of *hadith* is valid, it is a source of sharia and it is required to practice it accordingly. The only thing is that a *Ghareeb* or *azeez hadith* can abrogate it but it cannot abrogate a *mutawatir* text, which is Quran, or if there is a *mutawatir hadith*. This is according to the Hanafites, but Imam Shafi allows this, and *azeez* both are *wahi* like the *mutawatir*, so it can abrogate a *mutawatir* as well.

3. *Al Mashhur*

A *hadith* that is narrated by three or more narrators in each generation but fewer than the number of *mutawatir*.

There is another type of *Mashhur* as well. It is not based on the number of narrators but known to many people. People have quoted it many times, even though it is either *ghareeb* or *azeez* or even sometimes that is a *zaeef* one, but people quote it many times.

So when a *Mashhur hadith* is okay in *sanad* and text and has a contradiction with a *Ghareeb* or *azeez* one, then the *Mashhur* takes precedence, if the other two do not have any reason for its priority over this *Mashhur*.

4. *Al Mutawatir*

A *Hadith*, which is narrated by a large number of people in each generation.

There are very few *mutawatir*. However, as far as a particular subject is concerned then there are many *Mutawatir* as the same issue is there in so many *ahadith*. *Sahaba*, in general, practiced the subjects mentioned therein and later on that was the practice of innumerable people in each and every generation.

The ruling for a *mutawatir* is that it is as authentic as the Holy Quran in its sense and meaning. As the Quran is the word of Allah, while *hadith* is the word of the Prophet, this type of *hadith* can abrogate a ruling of the Quran if there is any. Some scholars did not count *Al Mashhur* as a type of *Aahad* but to them the *Hadith* is classified to these.

   i.   *Al Aahad*

  ii.   *Al Mashhur*

 iii.   *Al Mutawatir*

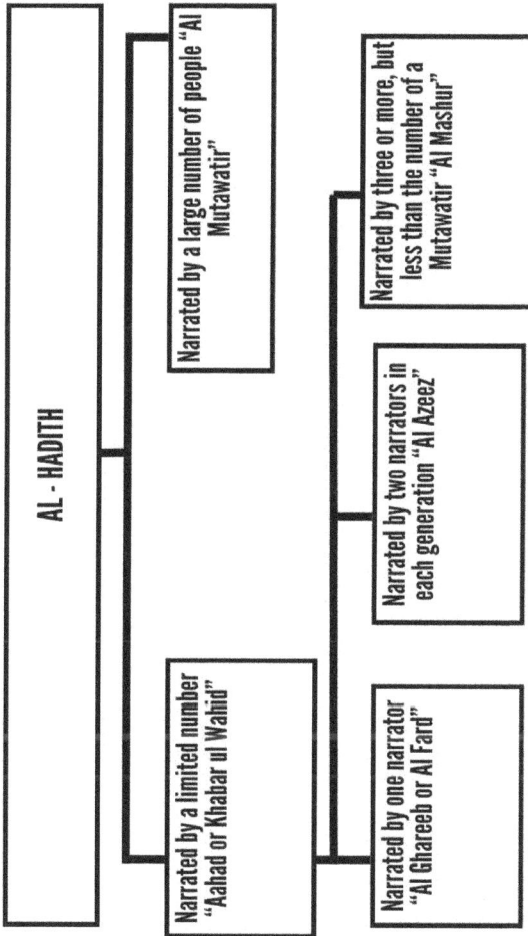

AL - HADITH

Narrated by a large number of people "Al Mutawatir"

Narrated by a limited number "Aahad or Khabar ul Wahid"

Narrated by three or more, but less than the number of a Mutawatir "Al Mashur"

Narrated by two narrators in each generation "Al Azeez"

Narrated by one narrator "Al Ghareeb or Al Fard"

Aahad is classified as:

1. AL MAQBOOL:

The truthfulness of this one is preferred.

2. AL MARDOOD:

Its truthfulness is not preferred.

Then *Maqbool* is further classified into four categories, which are:

1. *Saheeh* Li Dhatihi or *saheeh* on its own;

2. *Hasan Li Dhatihi* or *Hasan* on its own;

3. *Saheeh Li Ghairihi* or *Saheeh* due to something else;

4. *Hasan Li Ghairihi* or *Hasan* due to something else.

To know all these, even the Mardood, depends on knowing the *Saheeh Li Dhatihi* first. However, this science was not there at the time of *Sahaba* or even in the time of major *Tabieen*. Their base of action was what the Prophet was doing and then the practice of the *Sahaba*. However, when some people tried to support their ideas by quoting certain words calling them *ahadith aathar, Hasan Basri* said,

> *"Then we started asking them when they referred to something to name their teachers and the sanad. This was to stop them from quoting things baselessly."*

So *Saheeh Li Dhatihi* is a *hadith* that a person who is *adel* (possessed of a perfect memory) narrated, and it was transmitted with a continuous series of narrators without any *shuzooz* or *illah*. Five qualities must exist in a *Hadith* to be a *Saheeh Li Dhatihi*:

1) ADEL:

This is transparency. It means that the person is a pious Muslim who has never committed anything that is against the *Sharia* and who is possessed of piety, dignity, and decency. These qualities must be present at the time s/he delivers the *hadith*. If someone learned from the Prophet a thing when s/he was not a Muslim or when s/he was underage, but s/he was delivering the same when s/he was a Muslim or adult having other required qualities for narration, then the *hadith* is considered *saheeh*.

2) Having perfect memory or preservation in writing, as at that time they used to rely upon memory. This perfection means that whenever s/he wants to deliver the *hadith* s/he can do it without any confusion.

3) A continuous series of narrators that each and every student mentioned there has taken it from the teacher he mentioned, all the way back to the Prophet.

4) *Shuzooz* in a narrator means that even though he is reliable, the words he narrated are different from the words narrated by a narrator more reliable than him.

5) *Illat* or *illah* means a hidden reason that is only known to experts, like someone who narrates from a teacher but with some ambiguity, as he has taken this *hadith* directly or indirectly. Then if it is done by a narrator who is not a *mudallis* (one who hides the name of his own teachers because he was not a famous teacher in the field). There was a possibility that this narrator may have met that teacher to whom he attributes. In that case, this *hadith* is considered a *muttasil hadith* according to *Imam Muslim*. But according to Imam Bukhari, it must have been proven that they met more than once or twice. Otherwise, the *hadith* is not *muttasil* but *munqati* (a *zaeef hadith* with a discontinued chain of narration). When we know what a *hadith Saheeh Li Dhatihi* is, it is now easy to understand the other categories, as all types of *hadith* come from the lack of these qualities partially or as a whole.

HASAN LI DHATIHI

When all these qualities exist in a *hadith*. However, the only case is that of the memory of a narrator when it was weak, like ten percent or fifteen percent retention. Then the *hadith* is slightly lower in grade than a *Saheeh Li Dhatihi*. Regarding a base for *Sharia* that is like *Saheeh Li Dhatihi*, *saheeh* is preferred if there is any contradiction between them. *Imam Hakim* and *Ibn Hibban* both counted this type in the category of a *saheeh*.

SAHEEH LI GHAIRIHI

The same as *Hasan Li Dhatihi* if narrated through more than one chain. However, every chain had a narrator who had a slight weakness in memory. Then that *hadith* is elevated to the level of *saheeh*, but as this elevation is due to something else. So this is lower than *Saheeh Li Dhatihi* but higher than a *Hasan Li Dhatihi*.

HASAN LI GHAIRIHI

When the narrator is weak in memory, not correctly known in detail, or the narration chain is not a continuous one, that *hadith* itself is *zaeef*. If the same *hadith* is narrated through more than one chain it rises to the level of *Hasan Li Ghairihi*. It is lower than *Hasan Li Dhatihi*, but it is still a base and source of Sharia.

Note: If a *hadith* is *zaeef* because a narrator is a *Fasiq* (one who commits a major sin), or he lied at some point, then his *hadith* is *zaeef* and could not be elevated to the level of *hasan li ghairihi*, even if narrated through more chains. If a *Fasiq* learnt it when he was *Fasiq* but when he delivers it, he is no longer a *Fasiq*, then his *Hadith* is accepted and may be dealt with accordingly in the light of the rules of this science.

Note: When the *muhaddith* says a *hadith* is *saheeh* then it means that it has the required qualities. When a *muhaddith* says this is not *saheeh*, then it means that one or more qualities of *saheeh* are not there in its narration, but it does not mean that it is fake or a lie. Sometimes a *hadith* is *saheeh* according one *muhaddith* but not according to another. When they say

Asahh ul Asaaneed, it differs from group to group, and it depends on which chain is the most authentic according to them. So *Asahh ul Asaaneed,* according to *Imam Ahmad* and *Ishaq Ibn Rahwayh* are *Zuhri,* from *Salim,* from his father, *Abdullah Ibn Umar.* According to *Ibn ul Madeeni* and *Ali Ibni Fallas,* they are *Ibni Siren,* from *Ubaidah,* from Ali. According to *Iman Bukhari,* the most authentic chain is that of *Malik,* from *Nafi,* from *Ibn Omar.* A well-known critic of *hadith, Yahya Ibn Maeen,* said that it is *Aamash,* from *Ibrahim,* from *Alqamah,* from *Ibn Masud. Ibn Abi Shaibah* says it is from *Ali Zain ul Aabideen,* from *Hussein,* from *Ali,* and some other scholars said that *Asahh ul Asaaneed* is that of *Shafi,* from *Malik.* There are some *ulama* that said that a book of *hadith,* which is compiled based on the chain of *Malik,* from *Nafi,* from *Ibn Umar,* is the most authentic book. Then after that it is a book based on the chain *Hammad Ibni Salamah,* from *Thabit,* from *Anas,* and then in the third category is that one which is based on the chain of *Suhail Ibni Abi Salih,* from his father *Abu Salih,* from *Abu Huraira.*

Also they said that the utmost authentic *Hadith* is:

a. The one agreed upon by *Bukhari* and *Muslim* that they have put in their books;

b. Then what *Bukhari* has related;

c. What *Muslim* has narrated;

d. Then a *hadith* that qualifies the conditions for them both but they have not put it in their books;

e. Then a *hadith* that qualifies the conditions laid down by *Imam Bukhari* but he has not quoted it;

f. Then what is according to the requirements of the book of *Imam Muslim* but he has not put it in his book;

g. Then the one authenticated by other known critics of *hadith* like *Ibni Khuzaimah, Ibn Hiban,* and *Hakim.*

Note: The conditions or qualities for a *saheeh hadith* are the same well-known qualities according to the critics, but based on a deep study of the books of *Imam Bukhari* and *Muslim*, who say that according to *Imam Muslim* if a narrator is not a *mudallis*, and he narrates a *hadith* from a *Shaikh* in such a way that indicates that if he has heard it from him, and there was a possibility of their meeting, then that chain is a *muttasil*, and if it satisfies other requirements of the *saheeh* then it is *saheeh*. However, according to *Imam Bukhari* their meeting once or twice is a must for the continuation of a chain. When the *Muhaditheen* say *muttafaqun alaih* then it means that both *Bukhari* and *Muslim* have agreed upon this *hadith* in its *sanad* and *matan*. Before these two books the scholars agreed that the most authentic book in this regard is the *Mu'atta* of *Imam Malik*, but after these two were compiled, the *Jumhur* (absolute majority of the scholars) say that the book of *Imam Bukhari* is the most authentic. However, *Abu Ali Nisabur*, the teacher of *Imam Hakim* said,

> *"There is no more authentic book than the book of Imam Muslim."*

Moreover, *Imam Qurtubi* said, *"Both are equal."* When the *Muhaditheen* say *Saheeh Ul Isnad,* then that is better but lower in status than *saheeh*. The same way *Hasan Ul Isnad* is a little bit lower than *hasan*, so in *Hasan Ul Isnad* we can say that the chain is valid but in the text there is some *shuzooz* or *illah*. However, authentic scholars said that *Saheeh Ul Isnad* is equal to *Saheeh*. When they say *jayyid* then that *sadith* is *Hasan*, but according to *Imam Tirmizi* that is *saheeh* when he says *jayyid*. The terms *salih* and *qawi* is sometimes used for *saheeh* and sometimes for *hasan*. The word *maroof* for a *Hadith* is the opposite of *munkar*, and *Mahfouz* is the opposite of *shaz*, but the terms *thabit* and *mujawwad* according to some is for *saheeh* and *hasan*, while according to some others that are for *saheeh* only.

Imam Tirmizi, who is a known *muhaddith*, has his terms.

They are:

i.   *SAHEEH UN GHAREEBUN,*

ii. *HASAN GHAREEB UN LA NARIFUHU ILLA MIN HA DHA WAJHI,*

iii. *HASAN UN SAHEEHUN,*

iv. *HASAN UN GHAREEBUN.*

Now *Saheehun Ghareebun* is valid since a *Saheeh Hadith* could be a Ghareeb *Hadith* as well. When he says *Hasanun* he means according to us, even if he did not mention according to us, that is still meant; but when he says

> *"Hasanun Ghareebun La Narifuhu Illa Min Ha Dha Wajhin,"*

This is a contradiction, as Imam himself said that *hasan* has more than one chain while *Ghareeb* has only one chain. So we say that when the Imam looks at the qualities of *hasan* then to him more than one chain is a must, but when he says *Ghareeb* than he does not consider that. When he says *hasanun saheehun*, it could be that the *hadith* itself is *hasan*, but as it is narrated by more than one chain, so then it rises to the level of *saheeh*. *Hafidh Ibni Kathir* says maybe this is a position in between these two categories, while *Ibni Hajar* said, if that *hadith* has two different chains, then it could be *hasan* based on one and *saheeh* based on the other, and if it has only one chain then it means that this *hadith* is *saheeh* according to some critics and *hasan* according to some others.

A *hasan hadith* is one the *ummah* takes into consideration for their practice, and not only the *Fuqaha*, but also the *Muhaditheen* title it as a *saheeh* hadith. For example, the *hadith* when the Prophet was asked about whether seawater, which is full of dead organisms, was usable.

He said,

> *"Pure is its water, and hill [a word with two meanings, "pure" and "edible"] is its dead animals."*

111

The very narration of this *hadith* is *hasan* but when *Imam Bukhari* was asked about this *hadith*, he said it was *saheeh*. If a *hadith* is *zaeef* due to the lie of a narrator or his *fisq* (transgression of bounds), or he is *Majhooluzzat* (his whereabouts are unknown), then that *hadith* could never rise to the level of *hasan*. However, a *zaeef hadith* of a narrator whose memory was weak or confused, or *Mastoor ul Hall*, but it is narrated with another like narration, then it rises to the level of *hasan*. When we learned the types of *Hadith – E - Maqbool* so an idea about *Hadith – E - Mardood* came in mind that a *hadith* that is not of these types is *mardood* or *zaeef*. Essentially, that will be because of the lack of one or more of the qualities of *saheeh*. So a *Hadith – E - Zaeef"* is a *hadith* that lacks one or more of the qualities of a *Hadith – E - Hasan*. They are of various types: if the *sanad* does not have a continuation and a narrator or narrators have been dropped. Either it can be at the start of the *sanad* or from the end or the middle. or then there from we will have the following six types of *Hadith e Zaeef*;

a. *AL MUALLAQ*

b. *AL MURSAL*

c. *AL MUDAL*

d. *AL MUNQATI*

e. *AL MUDALLAS*

f. *AL MURSALUL KHAFI*

A. *AL MUALLAQ*

When the entire chain is dropped, or only the *Sahabi* is mentioned, or the *Sahabi* and *Tabiee* are mentioned, then the *Hadith* is called a *muallaq*. Academically we say this is *zaeef*, which is not as most of the *ahadith*, have its *sanad*. However, it is dropped in reference, making it short. Otherwise, *Imam Bukhari* relates *muallaq* as well, but all his *muallaq* are *saheeh*. Regarding a *muallaq* we are bound to find its *sanad* and then its status could be determined. *Imam Bukhari* has quoted *Muallaq*, but he has related the same as muttasil in another chapter except for 160 *Hadith*. *Hafiz Ibn Hajar* has written a book, <u>*At Taufeeq*</u>, where he has related all these *ahadith* as *muttasil*, and *Imam Muslim* has brought very few *muallaq* in his book.

Sometimes *Imam Bukhari* relates the same with a word ascertains that this is *saheeh*, meaning he used for the narration an active form of verb but he did not mention its *sanad* either to make it brief or for the topic concerned he has another *saheeh hadith*, or he has not taken it from his teacher, or he has a little doubt in the taking of this *Hadith*, or it was quoted in a talk. So this type we call it as attached to the condition of *Bukhari*, or that is *saheeh* according to others. That is valid to be the base of a *Sharee* issue, although there may be some discontinuation in its chain. *Imam Bukhari* does so either because he has heard this *hadith* of this particular *Shaikh* through another authentic narrator, but that *Shaikh* must know the *hadith*. He only quotes it if that such and such *Shaikh* has related the *hadith*. The second type is that one that he relates by using a passive voice like *"it is said"* or *"it is narrated,"* then it means that the said *hadith* is *saheeh* itself. For the acceptance of *muallaq*, there are requirements to get accepted:

i. It is in a book where the *muhaddith* limited himself to including the *saheeh hadith*.

ii. That is narrated only to make it brief and he has done that a lot.

iii. He learnt it from the *Shaikh* he mentioned but through another narration, but he is sure about that. Conversely, he doubted in his taking that from the said *Shaikh*, but he is sure that he has narrated the same, and the same *Shaikh* is his direct *Shaikh* as well.

iv. That *hadith* is *saheeh* but not based on his requirements.

v. The *hadith* is *hasan* but he made it *muallaq*. *Dari Qutni*, *Humaidi*, uses the term *muallaq* for similar *hadith* and then later on it became a frequently used term.

B. *AL MURSAL*

Is a *hadith* where a *Tabiee* dropped the *Sahabi* and attributed it directly to the Prophet (SAS). A *Tabiee* is one who has not seen the Prophet nor learnt from him. If a major *Tabiee* does this, the *hadith* is accepted as for sure he has dropped a *Sahabi* and all of them are *adel*. However, if a minor *Tabiee* did it, maybe he has dropped another *Tabiee* and a *Sahabi* as well, so that the *hadith* is not *mursal* but *muaddal*. The Jurists of *Kufa* say that even if a student of a *Tabiee* directly attributed a *hadith* to the Prophet, it is still called *mursal*, while according to *muhaditheen* that is *muaddal*. *Imam Hakim* sometimes adopts what these Jurists say and sometimes what the *muhaditheen* say. *Khateeb al Baghdadi* generalized this term and defined *mursal* as including *muaddal* and *munqati*. *Imam Sayuti* and *Ibnus Salah* preferred the first concept. *Ibn Abdul Barr* said that the direct attributes of minor *Tabieen* are *munqati* according to some scholars, but we say that *munqati* is a *hadith* where only one narrator is dropped, somewhere in the middle. Also, if more than one is dropped somewhere in the midst of the chain but not in the row, then that is also called *munqati*. There is another situation when a minor *Sahabi* attributes something to the Prophet something he has not personally heard or seen. So for sure he has dropped a major Sahabi, this is considered as *muttasil*. However, *Abu Ishaq* says we should investigate further because he might have learned it from a *Tabiee*. So he has dropped a *Tabiee* and a *Sahabi*, but we still say that is acceptable, and this type of narration of a minor *Sahabi* from a *Tabiee* is very rare. Then *mursal hadith* is accepted according to *Abu Hanifa, Malik, Fuqaha* of Iraq, and in a famous saying from *Ahmad* when that *Tabiee* is *adel*. Yes, if a *Tabiee* is proven that he is not *adel* then his narration is *mardood*, but not because that is *mursal* but because he is not *adel*.

The reason he narrates it as *mursal* are:

i.   The *Tabiee* has heard that *hadith* from a few *Sahaba*, so he does not mention their names;

ii.   He has taken it from a *Sahabi*, but he forgot from which one, so he does not mention;

iii. He does this to make it brief;

114

iv.   The *hadith* is famous amongst people, so it does not need someone to be mentioned;

v.   He quoted it in the discussion. Most *muhaditheen* and *Fuqaha* said that *mursal* is a type of *mardood* as it may be that the dropped one is someone other than a *Sahabi*.

This is also the saying of *Saeed Ibn ul Musayyab, Malik, Zuhari, Auzaee, Shafi* and *Ahmad* as *Hakim* said it. *Khateeb* also said that it is must to say about a narrator that he is *adel*, so when his name is not mentioned then, no one can say he will be an *adel* one.

Zuhari also said to *Ishaq Ibni Abi Farwah*

> "*How you relate hadith has no rein?*" *Imam Ahmad used to say that to narrate something mauqoof is better than its narration as mursal. Abdullah Ibd ul Mubarak said, "To recite a hadith without sanad is like climbing to the top of a roof without a ladder.*"

Imam Shafi said the base is Quran and Sunnah, if not then the *qiyas* and a *munqati* are nothing but only that of *Saeed Ibn ul Musayyab*. He used to accept his *mursal*, as most of his *mursal* are *musnad*. Other scholars said that Shafi accepts a *mursal* to prefer with, but not to make it a base for an issue, for his later purpose he puts the following conditions:

i.   Someone else has narrated the same *musnad*;

ii.   That *mursal* is the like of the saying of a *Sahabi*;

iii. Another one has also related it even he also relates it *mursal*;

iv.   The *Muftis* give fatwa on it;

v.   The one who relates *mursal* only relates it from someone trustworthy.

Imam Bukhari has not related a single *mursal* in his book. *Imam Muslim* has narrated 10 *mursals*, but its *sanad* is *musnad* as well, and he brought it as a support, not as a basis for an issue. However, *Imam Bukhari* said, *From Humaidi* that when a chain is ok up to a *Sahabi* even though if he is not mentioned by name then that is a base. *The Mursal* of a *Sahabi* is also a base as most probably he has learnt it from a major *Sahabi*, because if anyone of them has learnt a *Hadith* from a *Tabiee* then he mentions it. *Imam Sayuti* said a minor one who has seen the Prophet when he was a child, he is a *Sahabi*, but his *hadith* was *mursal*.

> *Abu Bakr Ibn ul Ath'ram asked Ahmad Ibni Hanbal that if a Tabiee said one Sahabi told him from the Prophet, is it a saheeh one? He said yes.*

We say that the *mursal* of a major *Tabiee* is accepted as he narrates from a *Sahabi* and all *Sahaba* are *adel*. Another reason they related *mursal* is that in the time of *Hajjaj,* the governor, they were not mentioning the name of Ali.

C. *AL MUNQATI*

This is a *hadith* where there are narrators dropped somewhere in the middle of the chain. However, *Imam Hakim* said one or two, so he included *mudal* in his definition as well. While according to others if more than one narrator is dropped but not in one place but different points then that is called *munqati* as well. However, *Imam Hakim* imposed a condition to the effect that the *hadith* has not been narrated through another chain of *muttasil*. Although we say that for academic purposes, we will say about its first chain that it is *munqati* but not the *hadith* itself. The experts and critics only know this. What *Dari Qutni* said about some *munqati* in the book of *Bukhari, Ibn Hajar* answered that *Bukhari* brought it as the narrator was not a *mudallis* and his meeting with the *Shaikh*, the fact that he has dropped is proven while *Imam Muslim* brought *munqati* after what he already narrated it as *muttasil*, so that is not a shortcoming.

D. *AL MUDAL*

This is a *hadith* where two or more narrators were dropped in one place from its narration chain consecutively, but *Ali Ibn ul Madeeni* said,

"A hadith in which two or more narrators are dropped continuously before the Prophet and not been narrated as a muttasil, anywhere, neither through this chain nor through another one."

Yes, the one which has been narrated by a *muttasil* one somewhere else is called *muaddal* according to *Hakim* only, and *Hakim* said it is essential to differentiate between a *Mu'dal Mausool* and *Mu'dal Ghair Mausool*. *Khateeb* said a *hadith* narrated by a student of a *Tabiee* directly from the Prophet was *mu'dal*.

E. *AL MUDALLAS*

F. *AL MURSAL UL KHAFI*

The difference between these two is that the first one is the narration from someone whom he has met, but he pretends that he has given him this *hadith*. While *Al Mursal Ul Khafi* is the narration from someone he has not met or met but never took a *hadith* from. However, he pretends that he has met in the first case, or he has learnt from him in the second one. So *Mudallas* is a *hadith*, which one narrates from a *Shaikh* he has learnt from him but not this *hadith*, but it could be explained either way. So his *hadith* him is *munqati* unless he used a word openly expressing that he has taken it from him. So if he is trustworthy, then this *hadith* is considered *muttasil*. This is called *Tadlees Ul Isnad*. Another type is *Tadleesu Shuyukh*, when he narrates from his Shaikh. However, he mentions a name or title of his by which he is not very well known. So if the *Shaikh* is trustworthy then this practice is *makrooh*, and if he is not trustworthy, then this is a prohibited practice.

These are the two famous types of *Tadlees*.

There are other types as well: if someone wants to study it, he should consult our book *Usool Ul Hadith* in Arabic.

The reasons for *Tadlees Ul Isnad* are:

i.   To make his *sanad* high;

ii. He missed taking some *ahadith* from that *Shaikh*. For *Tadlees ush Shuyukh* there are other reasons, and these are the reasons for *Tadless Ul Isnad* as well;

   a. That *Shaikh* was not trustworthy;

   b. That *Shaikh* was smaller in age;

   c. That *Shaikh* lived to an old age as some small people also got from him who is less in grade than this narrator;

   d. He has taken a bunch of *ahadith* from him, so he tries to have some varieties in quoting that *Shaikh*.

Then the narration of a *mudallis* is a type of *mardood* as a whole. But some other scholars said it may be analyzed, so wherever he has expressed that he has learnt it from that *Shaikh*, then that is *maqbool*. *Al Mursal Ul Khafi*, as we said before, is one who narrates with a word that could be explained either way. So if he is not a *mudallis*, and there was a possibility of his meeting with *Shaikh* according to *Imam Muslim* or According to *Imam Bukhari*, he must have met him once or twice, and then his *hadith* is *muttasil*. The critics know this or to the narrator himself that the said *hadith* is narrated through another chain having another link between this narrator and the said *Shaikh*. Then basically this type of *hadith* is from the category of *zaeef* as well.

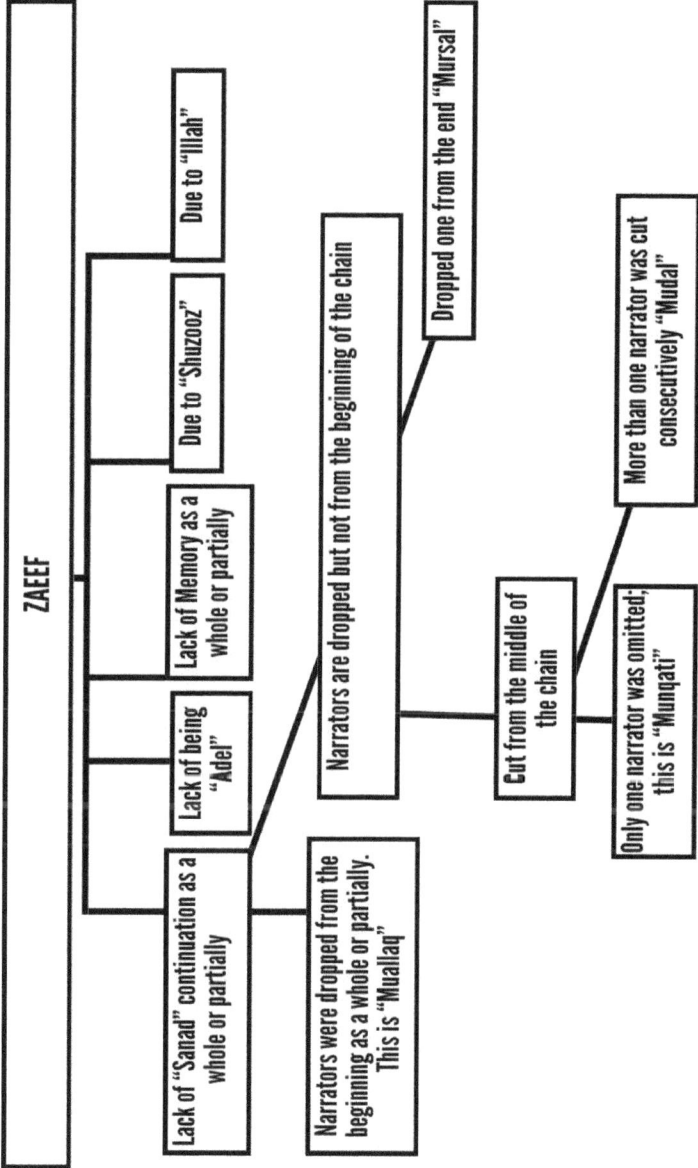

ZAEEF

- Lack of being "Adel"
- Lack of Memory as a whole or partially
- Due to "Shuzooz"
- Due to "Illah"
- Lack of "Sanad" continuation as a whole or partially
  - Narrators were dropped from the beginning as a whole or partially. This is "Muallaq"
  - Narrators are dropped but not from the beginning of the chain
    - Dropped one from the end "Mursal"
    - Cut from the middle of the chain
      - More than one narrator was cut consecutively "Mudal"
      - Only one narrator was omitted; this is "Munqati"

A *hadith* being *mardood* is a lack of an *adel* narrator. Critics talk about the character and piety of every narrator and describe whatever they find very precisely. So if they have not said anything about a narrator, then they call him *majhool*, that he is not known the way he has to be known. If they have said something regarding a narrator so that will be either that he lied, so his *hadith* is called *maudoo ("fake" or "fabricated")*. If he is only accused of lying but not it is not proven then he is called *matrook*, and if he is blamed for *fisq* he is *munkar* or *matrook*. And if he is making an innovation (*bid'at*) in *deen* or does not have decency then he is *zaeef*.

1. MAUDOO

This is not a type of *hadith* at all but some people tried to combine it with *hadith*. The critics talked about it; this is why it is included in this subject for academic purposes. The scholars said when something like this is quoted somewhere in a sitting then it is a must in the same sitting to be declared that this is *maudoo*.

In a *hadith* the Prophet said

> *"Anyone who intentionally told a lie about me may make his place in the fire [hell]."*

In some texts, this *hadith* is without the word *"intentionally,"* which means as long as one is not sure that the Prophet said it, he may not attribute it to him. Because of this, certain *Sahaba* related very few *ahadith* like *Abu Bakr, Abu Ubaidah, Abbas,* and *Zubair*. Some others were not recounting anything, like *Saeed Ibni Zaid,* and whenever *Anas* was narrating a *hadith*, he used to say after it,

> *"Or as the Prophet said."*

Ahadith were safe in the time of Sahaba, but when misguided people came, then lies began to circulate. The first one was a Jewish man named *Abdullah Ibni Saba*. He declared Islam seditious and attracted followers, and they started this fabrication, so the reason for this is as follows:

a) To support their own group through these fake sayings.

120

Ibni Abil Hadeed, a *Shiite,* said that in virtues the first ever fabricator was started by *Shiites. Hafiz Ibni Taimiyah* said, *the ignorant from Sunnis also started the same to counter them (Lisan ul Meezan).* On the other hand, the *Kharijites* (heretical) group does not do this, since lying is a major sin and according to them one becomes a disbeliever by committing a major sin. *But Hakim* narrated from *Ibni Lahee-aa* that a *Shaikh* from *Khawarij* who separated told me to look into these *Ahadith,* because whenever we liked a thing, we made a *hadith* for that. Also, the *Qadariyyah* and *Murji'aa* did the same.

b) POLITICS:

To connect with the rulers or to support their political ideology, some of them made up *hadith,* as the *"Shia"* did for *Ali,* and as some *Sunnis* did for *Abu Bakr* and *Umar.*

c) SECTARIAN PREJUDICE:

Unfortunately not only these misled groups but the followers of the four righteous *Imams* also put something in the virtues of their *Imam,* even though they had more than those virtues.

d) To gain some benefit from, or to slander, an enemy.

e) *AZ ZANDAQAH*

Is one who claims to be Muslim, but he tries to defame Islam. *Hammad Ibni Salamah* said that these types of people fabricated 12,000 *ahadith.* Because of this, before his execution *Abdul Karim Ibni Abil Auja* admitted that he had fabricated 4000 *ahadith.*

f) To tell people some strange stories to attract and exploit them.

Once *Ahmad* and *Yahya Ibni Maeen* both were praying in *Masjid Arrassafah,* and someone stood up and related a fake *hadith* with a strange story and attributed it to the Prophet through a narration of *Ahmad* and *Yahya.* They both looked at each other, and both of them were surprised that they knew neither this man nor this false *hadith.* After that, the man asked the people for money and received some, and the people left. Both of them came to him, and *Yahya* told him that he was *Yahya*, and this is *Ahmad* so if they wanted to fabricate something, please attribute it to someone else.

He said,

"Oh I had heard of you that he is a fool, but today I saw it." Yahya asked him, "How do you know I am a fool?" He said you think there is no other Yahya and Ahmad but only you both while I have written ahadith from nineteen Ahmad's and Yahya's. So Imam Ahmad covered his face with his sleeve and told Yahya let him go, so the person stood up and laughed at them.

g) NATIONAL OR RACIAL / ETHNIC PREJUDICE

h) To attract people towards something good they put a fake h*adith*.

Or to stop those from something bad they made some fake h*adith* giving a big fear. *Sayuti* relates from *Ibni Mahdi* that he asked *Maisarah* where from you brought these *ahadith* of virtues

"For the recitations of different surahs"? He said, "I made them to attract people to recite."

i) TO BECOME FAMOUS

Hammad a Nasibi and *Ibni Abi Dihyah* used to relate strange things.

Also, the group called *Karramiyyah* fabricated *ahadith* to support their point of view.

How could it be known?

i. By the admission and confession of the fabricators;

ii. Relating something from a *Shaikh* on a certain date, which is the date of the death of the same *Shaikh*;

iii.   Most of the *ahadith* by *Shiites* are in favor of *Ahlul Bait;*

iv.   A saying that is totally against *Quran* and *Sunnah;*

v.   A saying that is totally against reason or a proven history.

For the stated purpose to secure *ahadith,* the *ummah* imposed the following conditions:

i.   The condition of *sanad* along with the status and position of every narrator;

ii.   The history of who lived when and where;

iii.   To declare these types of people in words and writing so people may know them.

iv.   Through the signs of fakeness, which are known to the critics, and about which the critics compiled books.

2. AL MATROOK

This is a h*adith* whose chain is a narrator that has been accused of lying. That *Hadith* is only known through him and goes against the known rules and concepts. Also, the narrator is known for lying in casual conversation, or he is known for a lot of mistakes in narration or blamed for *fisq* or carelessness.

Khateeb narrates from *Ibn ul Mubarak* that he said,

"Hadith may be taken, but not from these four types of people:

i.   *One who makes a lot of mistakes in his narration;*

ii.   *A liar;*

iii.   *One who innovates in Deen and he invites to it as well;*

iv. *One who does not have proper memory and narrates from his memory."*

Abdur Rahman Ibni Mahdi would not take *hadith* from one who is accused of lying and who made a lot of mistakes. So the *hadith* of *matrook* may not be taken. *Matrook* is lower than *zaeef*, and *muza'af* is that *hadith*, which has been declared to be *zaeef* by some critics. Others did approve of that, so it is a little higher in status than *zaeef*.

3. *AL MUNKAR* and

4. *ASH'SHAZ.*

Ibni Hajar said that *munkar is a hadith in whose narration chain is a narrator whose fisq is known.* Also, he made many mistakes or as grossly negligent. But he differed from an authentic narrator in narration, and the opposite of *munkar* is called *maroof*. *Shaz* is the narration of an authentic narrator, but he differs from someone more authentic than him, or an authentic narrator narrated it differently than other authentic people. Imam Hakim stated that was the *Tafarrud* of an authentic one. But *Ibnus Salah* said,

> *"Then what about a saheeh hadith if narrated by only one authentic person?"*

Balqeeni answered this question that if that *hadith* is against the rules so *Shaz* is actually the narration of an authentic one different than the narration of a more authentic, and the narration of this more authentic is called *Mahfouz*. This *shuzooz* can be in the chain and can be in the text of *hadith*. The first one is like someone relating that *mursal* and another more authentic has narrated the same *mausool*, while the bad one is like someone who has added some extra words into a h*adith*, and he is less authentic than that one who has not brought those words, so the former is *shaz* and the latter is *Mahfouz*.

Majhool means that the narrator is not known, either at all or at least not in detail. This sometimes happens because someone goes by many names or has many titles, and when he is referred to by one of his lesser-known names or titles, people question who he is. Or his *riwayat* are so few that only one person has narrated from him, so he is not that famous or his name is not mentioned at all. So if a critic does not authenticate him then his *hadith* is *mardood* and called *zaeef*. This type of person is called *Majhool Ul Ain*. There is another one who is called "Mastoor Ul Hal" from whom two or more people relate but he has not been authenticated. His *hadith* is also called *zaeef*. A third category is *majhool uz zat*, when his name is not mentioned. Or if one of his names or titles is mentioned, but he is not known by that name or title, then he is called *mubham*, and his *hadith* is also *mardood* but authenticated. But we say that the best one in this regard is that the *hadith* of all these types mentioned above may not be categorized as *maqbool* or *mardood*, but *mauqoof* until he is authenticated. This is what Ibni Hajar said.

v.   The h*adith* of one who innovates knowing that to introduce a *bid'ah* (innovation) in *deen* is atrocious. *Bid'ah* is adopting a new practice thinking of it as a part of *deen* but it has no base or source in the *deen*. Then some *bid'ah* is "disbelief" like if one denied something in *deen*, which is from beliefs or he believed a thing that is not true. His *riwayat* is *mardood* and another type of *bid'ah* is *fisq* so the *riwayat* of such a person could be accepted if:

a) He does not call others towards that *bid'ah*;

b) He does not narrate what supports his *bid'ah* but some scholars say his *riwayat* may be rejected. Due to this, acceptance of his narration is his authenticity to his *bid'ah* as well.

NARRATION OF ONE HAVING NO

DECENCY

Even though this type of act, like walking in a bazaar and eating, is not a major sin but that is against dignity and later on because of this carelessness he could proceed towards sins, so that's why the *muhaditheen* have two opinions in this regard, whether his *riwayat* is *maqbool* or *mardood*.

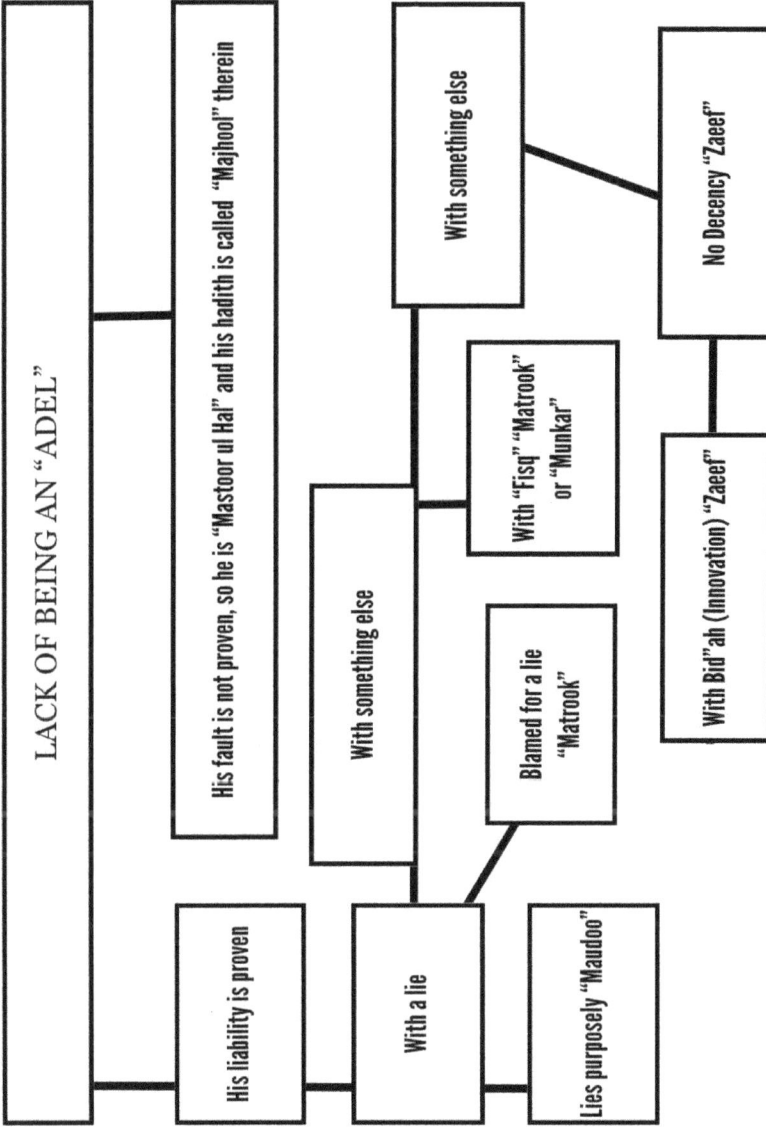

LACK OF BEING AN "ADEL"

His fault is not proven, so he is "Mastoor ul Hal" and his hadith is called "Majhool" therein

- With something else
  - No Decency "Zaeef"
  - With Bid"ah (Innovation) "Zaeef"
  - With "Fisq" "Matrook" or "Munkar"
  - Blamed for a lie "Matrook"

His liability is proven

- With a lie
  - Lies purposely "Maudoo"

LACK OF MEMORY

As we mentioned before that if the weakness of memory is 10% or 15%, then his *hadith* is *Hasan Li Dhatihi*. But if that is a lot then his h*adith* is considered *mardood* and that will be:

i. Making a lot of mistakes when he narrates;

ii. A lot of carelessness or negligence;

iii. His *fisq* is disclosed then his *hadith* is *munkar* or *matrook*;

iv. His memory is poor;

v. He is mixing up when narrating because he is old, so his brain is not working properly, or his sight is gone, or he has lost his books. His h*adith* will be *zaeef* but if narrated through another same like chain then it will rise to the level of *Hasan Li Ghairihi*.

vi. He has some confusion, so he makes a *mursal* into a *muttasil* or a *mauqoof* as *marfoo*, or he enters a *hadith* into another then his *hadith* is *muallal*.

He differs with authentic narrators, so he changes the order of the *sanad*, and then his *hadith* is *mudraj ul isnad*. If he mixes a *mauqoof* with *marfoo*, or a *maqtoo* with a *maqtoo*, then his *hadith* is called *mudraj ul matan*. If he disturbs the *sanad*, he puts the *Shaikh* in the place of the student and vice versa, so his *hadith* is *maqloob ul isnad*. And if he does the same in *matan* then that is a *maqloob ul matan*, and if he changes the narrator without reason then it is *mudtarab*. If he differs with an authentic one by changing the diacritical (dot) marks on letters, his *hadith* is *musah'haf*. If he changes the shape of a letter, then that is *muharraf*. If he has put an extra narrator in between even though the chain was a continuous one without that narrator, then this is called *Al Mazeed Fil Asaaneed*. If he is authentic and differed with another authentic narrator, then that *hadith* is *shaz*, and if he is *zaeef* differing with an authentic narrator then that is *munkar*.

AL MUDRAJ

Mudraj is said to be of two types:

1) In which its *sanad* is changed;

2) In its *matan* something is put;

    i.   The first one is when a group has related a *hadith* through different chains, and then one of them gathered the whole in one *sanad* without making the difference clear.

    ii.   A narrator has a distinct *sanad* for a *hadith*, and he has another *hadith* through another *sanad*. Some narrators narrate one of those two but put the second *hadith* as a whole or a part of it without making it clear.

    iii.   A narrator had taken a *hadith* from a *Shaikh*, but only a part of it. But through a narrator in between he relates the whole from the same *Shaikh* without clearing it with him.

    iv.   Same *Shaikh* has two *ahadith* with two different chains, but a student of his narrated both *Ahadith* through one "Sanad" or he narrated one but put a part of the other therein.

    v.   The narrator was narrating and was interrupted where he said something, which was not a part of that *hadith*, but the student thought it was a part of that *hadith*. These types of *mudraj* are based on study and research. The *mudraj ul matan* sometimes adds this at the very start of the *matan* or sometimes in the middle of it. That is little but more than the first one, and sometimes in its end and that is more. The narrator does this either to:

a. Explain a strange word in *hadith*;

b. To explain a *Shar'ee* rule;

c. To deduce a *Shar'ee* rule;

And this *mudraj* could be distinct:

a. As it is mentioned separately in another *hadith*;

b. The critics cited it as *mudraj*;

c. The very narrator said, *"This is from Shaikh so and so;"*

d. That thing could not be conceived that the Prophet had said it.

AL MAQLOOB

Changing of a word for another one from the *hadith* either in *sanad* or in *matan*, so *maqloob* is of two types:

1. MAQLOOB UL ISNAD

This is of two kinds:

a) A *Hadith* is very much known from a narrator but he replaced him with another narrator from the same generation, or he has changed the *sanad* as a whole. If the narrator does so purposely, then it is said, *"He is stealing ahadith."*

b) He changed the name of father to son and vice versa, like instead of *Ka'b Ibni Murrah*, he said *Murrah Ibni Ka'b*.

2. MAQLOOB UL MATAN

This is a change in the *Matan* of *hadith*.

There is a third category also where in one *hadith* the same two things are done. Then if this is for the purpose of a test, then that is all right. If that is done with some other intention, then that is considered *maudoo* as it changes the meaning and the sense and disturbs the religious concept. If it was a mistake, it is not a sin, and if it happens to him often, then his *ahadith* are considered *zaeef*.

3. AL MUDTARAB

A *hadith* that is narrated in different ways but each one, is an authentic way. But the various ways contradict each other in such a way that no correction could be made. No preference may be given to one of them over the others, nor we can say that one of them has abrogated the others. So if there is any substantial reason to prefer one of them, then the preferable one is the accepted one, and the other one is either *munkar* or *shaz*. If there is a possibility of correction, then both may be practiced.

Mudtarab is also of two types:

1) MUDTARAB UL SANAD

This is narrated by one person but some people have narrated it as a *mursal*. Some others as a *mausool* and there is no possibility of *tarjeeh* (preference) or correction.

2) MUDTARAB UL MATAN

This is when the words of *hadith* differed, so some of them related it with different words than the others. This *idtirab* indicates the weakness of accurate preservation but some of that will still be *hasan* or even *saheeh* like an *idtirab* in the name of the narrator and the name of his father.

4. AL MUSAH'HAF

5. AL MUHARRAF

The *musah'haf* one is the *hadith* where the diacritical marks of a letter were changed. In the case of a *muharraf*, the shape of a letter was changed.

If it was minor, then it does not affect the authenticity. But if there are many, then it means that either he is careless, or he makes many mistakes. The expert critics know this. Bad memory means that his proper narration could not be preferred on the opposite side, meaning he is 50/50. If this happening since he started narrating *ahadith* then his *hadith* is considered *shaz*. If it happened to him due to his old age, or vision loss or because he has lost his books then we have to differentiate between what he narrated before that and what he narrated after that. The first category is accepted; the second one is *mardood* and if we could not differentiate regarding *hadith*, then that is *mauqoof* until we find out its time and status.

LACK OF MEMORY

- **Lots of mistakes**
- **Lots of carelessness**
  - Matrook or Munkar
- **Differs in the authenticity**
  - Bad Memory, as his mistakes and the right approach, is 50/50 "Zaef"

Confusion (Wahm) makes a mursal one a mausool or a mauqoof one a marfoo or he enters one hadith into another mullal

- He is authentic but differs from an extra authentic "Shaz."
- He puts extra name in the chain even though the chain was complete "Al Mazeed"
- He is Zaeef and differs with an authentic one "Munkar"

Mix up, as his mind is disturbed or his sight is gone or he lost his books "Zaef"

If it is narrated through another same like "sanad" then it elevates it to the level of "Hasan Li Ghairihi"

- Changes the shape of the letter "Musharraf"
- Changes the dots on letters "Musah'haf."
- He changes the places of different names or words "Maqloob"
- Changes without reason "Mudtarab."
- Mudtarab us Sanad -Someone narrated it as mursal and someone as Mausool while the chain is one
- Mudtarab ul Matan- When two Matans contradicted, and the chain is one

- He puts something therein the hadith, which is not a part of it "Mudraj"
- Mudraj Ul Isnad
- Mudraj Ul Matan
- Maqloob ul Isnad - If the change is in the sanad
- Maqloob ul Matan - If the change is in the text of hadith

MUDRAJ

Mudraj ul Isnad

- In the middle and that is little but more than the first one
- In the beginning and that is very concise
- When a group related a hadith through various chains, then one of them gathered it in one chain and did not mention the variety
  - When one narrator related one part of a hadith and another one another part and their common student related both parts on the sanad of the first shaikh only or the second shaikh only
  - When he took part of a hadith from one shaikh and then another part from the shaikh of that shaikh, and later on he related the whole from this great shaikh
  - As he was taking a hadith from a Sheikh, the Sheikh makes a pause for some reason and then said something but the student thought it was also part of that hadith
  - When a narrator has two Ahadith through two different chains. Then his student related both through one chain or he related a hadith with his individual chain, but he added to it from the matan of another, which is not through this chain

Mudraj ul Matan putting words of a shaikh in the hadith without making any distribution

- At the end of the hadith and that is more
- At the end of the hadith and that is more

The nonexistence of *illah* is another condition in *saheeh*. If the *illah* exist then the *hadith* is *mardood*, if someone has *wahm* then his *hadith* is called *muallal*. So that is a *hadith* where an *illah* is found even though apparently it was looked as without *illah*. But that *illah* must have degraded its status and if not, then it is called neither *muallal* nor *mardood*. For example, if a *mausool* is narrated as *mursal* but by an authentic narrator. This is a very tough subject, and only the skillful people like *Ibn ul Madeeni, Ahmad,* and *Dari Qutni* know this. Then this *illah* sometimes in *sanad* cannot degrade the *matan* as he changed an authentic narrator by another authentic narrator.

AL MAZEED FI MUTTASILIL

ASAANEED

This is when a narrator is added in the middle of the *sanad* even though the sanad was *muttasil* without that name. To reject this type of combining has its conditions:

i. A narrator who does not have this addition is more authentic than that one who does;

ii. The narrator himself expressed that he has taken it from a specific *Shaikh*. Otherwise this addition is accepted, and the chain that does not have this added name is considered as a *munqati*. That *munqati* would be a type of *Al Mursal Ul Khafi*.

Some of them said that the chain that does not have that added name. If in the same place as the addition the narrator used the word *"an"* then it could be *munqati*. However, if he has expressed his hearing from the *Shaikh*, then we can say that maybe he had taken it from that *Shaikh* through another Shaikh and later on he got it from him directly.

TAFARRUD OF THE NARRATOR

Tafarrud means he narrated it different than other narrators. Then either he is authentic or *zaeef*. If he is authentic, either he differed in an extra authentic narrator or not. The first one is called *shaz* while the second one is *saheeh*. If he is *zaeef* and differed from an authentic narrator, then his *hadith* is *munkar*. If he did not dissent, but his memory is a little bit weak, then his *hadith* is *hasan*, and if that is very weak, then his *hadith* is also called *shaz*.

Note: A *hadith* that is *zaeef*, is taken into consideration if its weakness is not a unanimous decision by the critics. Alternatively, if that *hadith* has been taken into account for practice by the early generations while the weakness is because of a narrator later on so for virtues, that is acceptable.

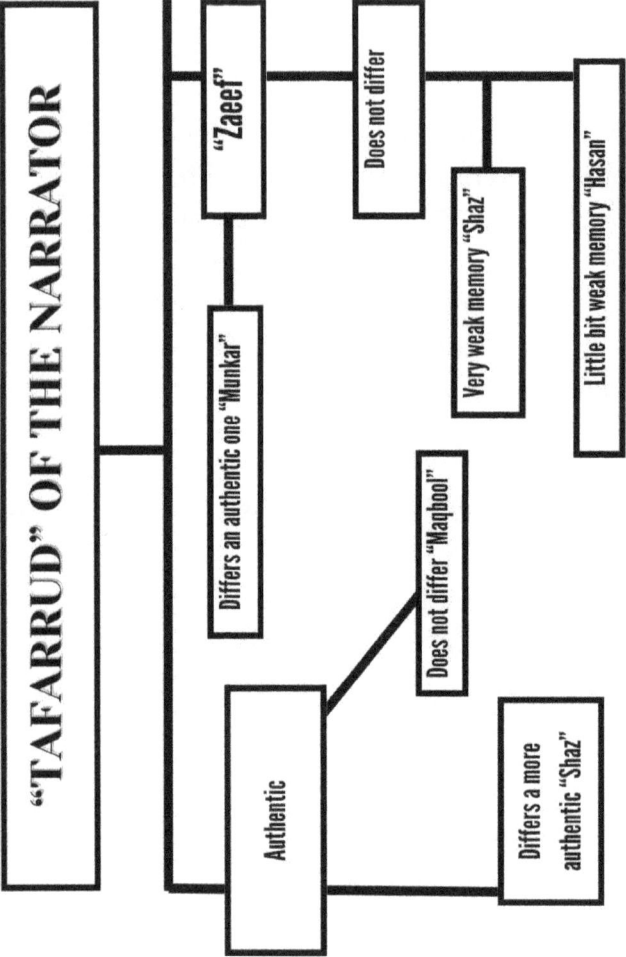

CRITICAL DISCUSSION OF THE

NARRATORS

Talking about someone in his absence is not allowed in Islam. This is called back stabbing and is especially heinous especially if the subject is dead.

The Prophet said,

> *"That abstain from his bad and appreciate his good deeds,"*

but here the critics talk about some of those who passed away in a good way but in other ways about some others. This is not only allowed but it is their duty as the Prophet said,

> *"To talk about someone in his absence to protect the life, property, or honor of another is exempted."*

While here there is the case of *deen* and *Sharia.* It relates to the life, properties, honor and even beliefs of others and an extent to the great and supreme honor of the Prophet of Allah so no wrong may be attributed to him. So this is a must to disclose the position of a narrator whether he is just, trustworthy, or not. Now this status of a narrator could be based upon:

I. The verification of the authentic critics;

II. Based on his good fame in the eyes of scholars like the four Imams and the popular *muhaditheen*.

To verify someone, the critics do not need to give the details as to how he is considered just and trustworthy. The required qualities are many so then word of verification is enough, but to put a finger on someone, detail is necessary. For the said purpose, the testimony of one critic is enough. As for narration, it is not necessary for a narrator to be male. One woman who is trustworthy is enough for narration; even a slave can narrate. although he cannot testify, even someone who is punished for *qazaf* (a false charge of fornication) is accepted after he repents, even though his testimony is not accepted according to *Imam Abu Hanifa.*

Allama Zahabi said,

> "No woman narrator was a matrook nor has been blamed."

Then this verification has different categories, some of which are higher than the others. In the same way the critics are different, some of them are very difficult to verify while some others are lenient. Regarding *bid'ah*, the balanced stand is that of *Imam Bukhari* and *Imam Muslim* as they narrated from certain narrators from a particular sect. *Imam Sayuti* said in *At Todreeb* that in *Bukhari's* narrators are 15 *Murji'aa*, 7 *Nawasib*, 26 *Shiah*, and 28 *Qadaris* and *Khawarij*, while these sects are known for their *bid'at.*

AT TAHAMMULU WAL ADA

Every *hadith* needs a link. As we have said before that if someone has learned something from the Prophet when he was young, or he was not a Muslim at that time, but he delivered that after his maturity and after his conversion then that is ok. Mostly the students take *ahadith* from their teachers, either the *Shaikh* reads it, and they take it. The student reads it, and the *Shaikh* confirms, verifies, or corrects. However, there are some other ways as well like someone asks a *Shaikh* to give him *ijazah* (permission). So even though he has not learned from him now, he can narrate from him.

BOOKS OF *HADITH*

As we have discussed in detail in our book *The Authenticity of Hadith* that *Sahaba* used to give priority to memorizing. However, still used to write *ahadith* as well, it was the case of *Tabieen*. *Imam Muhammad Ibni Muslim Ibni Shahab Az Zuhari* by the order of Khalifa *Umar Ibni Abdul Aziz* did the official compilation of *hadith* in the 100th year after *Hijra*. Then later on *Imam Malik* wrote his *Mu'atta*, then *Imam Muhammad* wrote his *Mu'atta*, and after that generation the *muhaditheen* compiled *ahadith* in different ways.

The *muhaditheen* categorized that as follows:

1. AL JAMI

That type of book that includes all eight types of subjects as:

    i.   *THE AQA'ID*

    ii.   *THE AHKAM*

    iii.   *THE SIAR*

    iv.   *THE AADAAB*

    v.   *THE TAFSEER*

    vi.   *THE FITAN*

A few examples of *jami* are; the book of *Imam Bukhari* and the book of *Imam Muslim*. Also the *jam* of *Abdur Razaq as San'aani*, the book of *Thawri*, and the book of *Ibni Oyainah*. From amongst these types, we want to tell you a little bit about the first two;

1) *SAHEEH BUKHARI*

Its actual name is <u>*Al Jami Ul Musnad as Saheeh Min Umoori Rasoolilah Wa Sunanihi Wa Ayyamihi.*</u> Before the compilation of this book the <u>*Mu'atta*</u> of Imam Malik was considered the extra authentic book in *ahadith*. However, that had the *mauqoof* and *maqtoo* Aathaar of Sahaba and Tabieen as well. While this only has the *ahadith* of the Prophet, in *ahadith* this is the extra authentic book. The *muhaddith* was *Imam Abu Abdullah Muhammad Ibni Ismail Ibni Ibrahim Al-Bukhari al Ju'fi Al Yamani.* He was born in 194 (After Hijra) and passed away in 256 (After Hijra). He started his education in hadith when he was less than ten years of age and then he traveled constantly for that purpose for 16 years to *Makah, Madina, Sham, Misr,* and *Iraq.* He learned *ahadith* from more than 1000 *Shuyukh* and got six hundred thousand *ahadith* before he was less than 18 years old. Even students started taking *ahadith* from him. He was a pious, trustworthy, just, integrated *Imam*, and scholar of *ahadith.*

He compiled several books, including:

V. *KITAB DUAFA AS SAHGEER*

VI. *AL ADAB UL MUFRAD*

VII. *JUZU RAFIL YADAIN*

VIII. The Famous Book *AL JAMI US SAHEEH*

He started the compilation of this book in Makah and spent 16 years on it. He conducted perfect research on each and every *hadith*. After compilation, the authentic scholars verified it. Every *hadith* in his book is *saheeh*. It is based on his thorough research as he said,

> *"I have not put here but only saheeh, and have left a lot of saheeh as well."*

Hafiz Ibn Hajar said that there are a total of 9,082 *ahadith* including *muallaq* and *mutabi*, while without *muallaq* and *mutabi* there are 7397, and when we drop the repeated *ahadith*, we are left with 2602. He divided his book into 97 chapters with 3405 sub-chapters. In his lifetime, 90,000 students learned this book from him. Different scholars have explained his book in different eras.

2) *SAHEEH MUSLIM*

According to *Jumhur* this is the second book in status while to some scholars this is superior to that of the book of *Imam Bukhari*. *Imam Muslim* was born in 204 A.H. and passed away in 261 A.H. His name is *Muslim Ibn ul Hajjaj Al Qushairi*. He was an *Imam, Hafiz*, and a great scholar of *ahadith*. He began studying *ahadith* when he was only 12 years old and began traveling to conduct his research when he was 14. He traveled to *Makah, Madina, Ray, Iraq, Misr, Sham, Khurasan*, and other places. He studied under more than 200 *Shuyukh* and collected more than 300,000 *ahadith*. He has written a few books beside this one like:

I. *TABQAT UT TABIEEN*

II.   AL ILAL

III.   AL JAMI UL KABEER

IV.   AUHAM UL MUHADITHEEN

He spent 15 years in the compilation of this *saheeh*. He completed it in 250 A.H. He declared that he did not include anything he could not back up with evidence, or leave anything out. He presented his book to scholars like *Hafiz Abu Zur'ah* and they verified it.

He says,

> *"I put here only those ahadith the Muhaditheen unanimously approved it as saheeh."*

One of his students *Ahmad Ibni Salamah* said that the total number of *ahadith* in this book is 12,000, and *Abu Quraish Al Kohistani* said that without the repeated ones its number is 4,000. *Imam Sayuti* said that all his *ahadith* are agreed upon by *Imam Bukhari* in his book as well, but there are only 320 that are not there in the book of *Bukhari*. He wrote this book without putting the chapters. So scholars like *Qazi Ayaz, Hafiz Mundhiri,* and *Imam Nawawi* put these headings. There are 54 of these headings. He wrote an excellent preface at the beginning, and that is considered the first ever book in <u>Usool Ul Hadith</u> and critical discussion. In his book, there are only 14 *muallaqat* but *Ibnus Salah* said there were 12 and *Ibni Hajar* said six only, as in the remaining six he made the names of his *Shaikh* ambiguous. In 40 *ahadith*, his *sanad* is *Aali* (High) than his *Shaikh Imam Bukhari*. He put only 192 *Mauqoof* and *Maqtoo* in his book. He very rarely repeats a *hadith*. Also, he mentioned all the chains of one *Hadith* in one place. Putting *ahadith* in order is excellent in his book, and that is the base of its priority given by some scholars over the book of Bukhari. Like the *Saheeh* of *Bukhari*, the scholars wrote *Shurooh* (Commentaries) on *Saheeh* Muslim as well.

2. AS SUNAN

This is a type of book where the compiler compiled this book in the same order of topics as *fuqaha* (jurists) did. There are many *sunan*, but here we will talk about those four, which are counted as *sihah sittah* with the books of *Bukhari* and *Muslim*.

Note: *Sihah* is the plural of *saheeh* but it does not mean that only these books are *saheeh* and others are not. Also, it does not mean that each hadith in these books is *saheeh* as there are *zaeef* in *sunan* as well.

i.   SUNAN I ABI DAWUD

His name is *Suleiman Ibn ul Ash'ath As Sijistani*. He was born in 202 A.H. and passed away in 273 or 275 A.H. He was an *Imam, Hafiz,* and *faqeeh*. He first studied in his hometown and then he traveled to *Makah, Madina, Iraq, Sham, Misr,* and other places. He has more than 300 *shuyukh* to his name. He was a student of *Ahmad, Yahya Ibni Maeen*, and was the teacher of *Tirmizi* and *Nasa'e*. He collected 50,000 *ahadith*. He wrote this *sunan* and also another book, *Maraseel*, and a third one by the name of *Masa'il I Ahmad*. The number of *ahadith* in his book is 5274. He has included *saheeh* and the *hasan*. Also, there are a few *zaeef* as well. Mostly he put there the *ahadith*, which the *fuqaha* took into consideration for *fiqh*. He does not repeat a *hadith* but only a few times where it is needed. The critics said when *Abu Dawud* keeps quiet about a *hadith* then that is *saheeh* according to him or Hasan at least. His book also has the commentaries by the scholars.

ii.   SUNAN UT TIRMIZI

This book is also called *Al Jami* and *As-Saheeh*. Imam Muhammad Ibni Isa at Tirmizi* was born in 209 A.H. and passed away in 279 A.H. He was also an *Imam* and *Hujjah*. He studied under *Imam Bukhari* and others. He also traveled to *Hejaz, Khurasan, Iraq,* and many other places. After the compilation of his book, he presented it to the scholars, and they appreciated it. Like his *Shaikh Abu Dawud*, he also put the *ahadith* that were considered by the *Fuqaha* in his book. He also speaks about most of the *ahadith* whether they were *Saheeh* or *Hasan* or otherwise.

He also refers to the *ahadith* relating to that chapter. His book also has a few *shurooh*.

iii.   *SUNAN I NASA'E*

His name is *Ahmad Ibni Shuaib An Nasa'e.* He was born in 215 A.H. and passed away 303 A.H. He was an *Imam, Hafiz,* and a scholar of *hadith* and *fiqh.* He traveled for *Hadith* to *Hejaz, Iraq, Sham, Misr,* et cetera. To verify a *Hadith* he has his strict conditions.

His bibliography includes:

a) AS SUNAN UL KUBRA

b) AS SUNAN UL SUGHRA

c) AL MUJTABA

d) AD DUAFA

e) AT TAFSEER

f) AMAL UL YAUMI WAL LAILAH

His book is known as *Sunan I Nasa'e,* which he condensed from *As Sunan ul Kubra.* It is also called *As Sunan ul Sughra* and *Al Mujtaba.* In *sunan,* this book is more authentic. The majority of its *ahadith* are also there in the book of *Imam Bukhari* and *Imam Muslim.* This book has *saheeh, hasan,* and some *zaeef.* He mentions a difference in different narrators of a *hadith* and also mentions the status of narrators. His book also has a few *shurooh.*

iv.   *SUNAN-I-IBNI MAJA*

His name is *Muhammad Ibni Yazid Ibni Maja Al Qazweeni.* He was born in 209 A.H. and passed away in 273 A.H. He was an *Imam, Hafiz,* and scholar of *hadith* and *Usool Ul Hadith.* He also traveled to *Hejaz, Misr, Ray, Basrah,* and Baghdad to study *ahadith.*

v. His written books are:

a) *AS SUNAN*

b) *AT TAREEKH WAT TAFSEER*

This book is the sixth of *sihah* while to some other scholars the sixth book is *mu'atta*. *Ibni Hajar* said the *Sunan of Darimi* was the sixth one. There are 37 chapters and 1500 sub-chapters in *Sunan Ibni Maja*. The order in which he put the chapters is remarkable. This book has some *zaeef*, *munkar*, and a few *maudooaat* as well. There are 4341 *ahadith* in this book. Almost 3002 of his *ahadith* can be found in the five previous books. From the remaining 1339 *ahadith* 428 are *saheeh*, 613 are *zaeef*, and 99 are either *munkar* or its *sanad* is very feeble and frail. His book has a few *shurooh* as well.

3. *AL MUSANNAF*

This type of book also has the same order as *Sunan*, but it includes *mauqoof* and *maqtoo* as well, and even the religious verdicts of the third generation.

A few of this type are:

i. *MUSANNAF OF HAMMAD IBNI SALAMAH*

ii. *MUSANNAF OF WAKEE IBN UL JARRAH*

iii. *MUSANNAF OF ABDUL RAZZAQ IBNI HAMMAM*

iv. *MUSANNAF OF BAQEE IBNI MUKHALLAD*

v. *MUSANNAF OF IBNI ABI SHAIBAH*

4. *AL MUSTADRAK*

As we mentioned before, some compilers like *Bukhari* and *Muslim* imposed conditions on their compilations. Later on some other compilers compiled their books based on their conditions but they did not put those *ahadith* in their book. A few of these types are; *Mustadrak of Hakim*, who put in *ahadith* according to the conditions of both *Bukhari* and *Muslim* or according to the conditions of anyone of them. He also put *ahadith*, which are s*aheeh* according to *Hakim* himself.

5. *AL MUSTAKHRAJ*

In this type of book the compiler put a book of *hadith* in front of him and then he relates the same *ahadith* through his chains of narration. Yes, he gets together with the author of the book either at the level of his *Shaikh* or even above that.

There are a few *Mustakhrajat* such as those of:

I. *ABU NAEEM AL ASBAHANI*

II. *ABU BAKR AL BURQANI*

III. *IBN UL AKHRAM*

IV. *AL ISMAILI*

V. *AL GHATREEFI*

VI. *IBNI ABI ZUHAL*

VII. *ABU AWANAH*

VIII. *AL HAIRI*

IX. *ABU HAMID AL HIRAWI*

6. *AL MU'ATTA*

This is almost like *As Sunan* and *Al Musannaf*, and a few are that of:

I.   *IMAM MALIK IBNI ANAS*

II. *IMAM MUHAMMAD IBNI HASAN*

III. *IBNI ABI ZIB*

IV. *AL MAROZZI*

The *Mu'atta* of *Malik* is the famous one in this regard. The compiler is *Imam Malik Ibni Anas,* who was born in 93 A.H. and passed away in 179 A.H. He was an *Imam, Hafiz, muhadith* and *faqeeh*. This book is the first ever book compiled in *Hadith i Saheeh*, but he also put there the *mauqoof, maqtoo*, and the *Fatwas. Imam* has chosen this from 100,000 *Ahadith* and compiled it in 40 years. *Allama Abhari* said that there were 600 *musnad*, 222 *mursal*, 613 *mauqoof* and 285 *maqtoo ahadith*. The *Aathaar* in this book total 1720. Because of the deductions of the *Imam* in his book some scholars said that this is a book of *fiqh*. Then *Hafiz Ibn Abdul Barr* has connected all its *marasil* and *Munqati* except four, but *Ibnus Salah* connects those. This book also has a few *shurooh*.

Other types of books are compiled based on the names of *Sahaba* or the beginning words of the *hadith* or even on a known part of it and these are:

1. *AL MUSNA*:

In this type they have collected *ahadith* based upon the names of *Sahaba*. Then the *Sahaba* have been taken as their history of accepting Islam or based on their tribes or cities or alphabetically. There are almost 100 *musnads* but a few famous ones are:

i.   *MUSNAD I AHMAD IBN HANBAL*

ii. *MUSNAD I HUMAIDI*

iii. *MUSNAD ABU DAWUD AT TAYALASI*

iv. *MUSNAD ASAD IBNI MUSA*

v. *MUSNAD MUSADDAD IBNI MUSARHAD*

vi. *MUSNAD ABD IBNI HUMAID*

vii. *MUSNAD I ABU YALA*

The *Musnad of Imam Ahmad Ibni Hanbal* is the famous and big one. He was born in 164 A.H. and passed away in 241 A.H. He was an *Imam* in h*adith* and *fiqh* both. He collected all 750,000 *ahadith* and memorized them. He compiled his book in such a way that he put the *ahadith* of 10 major *Sahabas*, who were given the glad tidings of paradise here and then based on the positions of other *Sahaba* or their cities or tribes. He brought *ahadith* from 904 *Sahaba* and collected there almost 40,000 *ahadith*, out of which 10,000 are repeated. In this book, there are *saheeh*, *hasan*, *zaeef*, and *munkar*. Most *zaeef* and *munkar* are in that part and were put there by his son *Abdullah*. Some scholars said that there are 17- *maudoo hadith* also in *musnad*, but *Ibni Hajar* said *Maudoo* are only 3 or 4 only. Yes, the *Zaeef* he put there as *mutabi*.

2. MU'JAM-

The kind of *Hadith* book where the *Ahadith* are put based on the order of *Sahaba* or the basis of *Shuyukh* or reference, and mostly these are alphabetical. The famous *Mu'jam* are those written by *Imam Tabrani* and these are:

I. *AL MU'JAM UL KABEER*

This is based on the name of *Sahaba* except *Abu Huraira* as he compiled it separately. It is said that there are 60,000 *ahadith* in this *Mu'jam*.

II. *AL MUJAM UL AUSAT*

This is based on the name of his own *shuyukh*, of which there are 2000. There are almost 30,000 *ahadith* in this one.

III.   *AL MU'JAMUS SAGHIR*

This one he wrote from nearly 1000 of his *shuyukh*, mostly one hadith from each one. There is another *mu'jam* of *Ahmad Ibni Ali Al Hamdani* and another of *Ahmad Ibni Ali al Moosali*.

Note: As *musnad* and *mu'jam* are compiled based on *Sahaba*, so we say that all *Sahaba* are just, integrated, and trustworthy. They are more than 100,000 in number. A *Sahabi* is one who saw the Prophet, believed in Him, and died a Muslim. It does not matter whether he stayed a long time or for a short period with the Prophet (SAS). *Ibni Sa'd* categorized them into five classes and Hakim into 12 categories. The best amongst them are *Abu Bakr, Umar, Uthman,* and *Ali,* in that order. The remaining 6 out of 10, and then who attended *Badr,* then Sahaba of *Uhud,* then of Hudaibiyah. The last of those who died in 100 A.H. was *Amir Ibni Wathilah al Laithi. Abu Huraira* has narrated 5374 *ahadith* and more than 300 people narrated from him. *Abdullah Ibni Umar* narrated 2630 *Ahadith, Anas Ibni Malik* 2286, *Aisha* 2210, *Abdullah Ibni Abbas* 1660 and *Jabir Ibni Abdullah* 1530. *Masruq* said this knowledge of *Sahaba* was with *Umar, Ali, Ubai, Zaid Ibni Thabit, Abu Darda,* and *Ibni Masud. Ibni Abbas* is the one who made many *fatwas* in plenty. *Ibni Hazm* said that 750 *Sahabas* mostly relate *ahadith,* while 150 of them have *fatwas.*

MUKHTALIF UL *HADITH*

As we said before, there are three types of *ahadith*, but in *aahad* there will sometimes be a contradiction. When this happens, and there is a possibility of taking both into consideration for practice, then both may be practiced. If not, then if the date of each one is known for sure then the later one will take precedence over the earlier one. However, this abrogation can be known through the *hadith* itself or the saying of a *Sahabi* or his practice, and he is the narrator of the abrogated one or by *ijma* or by date. Moreover, if the date is not known then they are known to prefer one of those *ahadith* to the other. There are 110 reasons according to *Allama Iraqi*, 150 according to *Hazimi*, and 100 according to *Sayuti*. This subject is mostly the subject of *Fuqaha*.

The details are there in our Arabic book *Usool Ul Hadith*. As we mentioned, these *Muhaditheen* traveled and spent a lot to collect and preserve *ahadith. Jabir Ibn Abdullah* traveled one month for one hadith, and *Abu Ayub* traveled from Medina to *Misr* for only one hadith. *Imam Zuhari* studied for 20 years with *Saeed Ibn ul Musayyab*, while *Yahya Ibni Saeed Al Qatan* spent ten years with *Shobah. Imam Malik* took ahadith from 900 *shuyukh, Hisham Ibni Abdullah* from 1700, *Ibn ul Mubarak* from 1100, and *Imam Abu Hanifa* from 4000. *Nafi Ibn Abdullah* stayed with *Imam Malik* for 40 years for this purpose, coming to him three times every day. *Abu Naeem* learned it from 800 *shuyukh. Malik* says,

> *"My Shaikh Rabee'a spent whatever he had, and he even sold his house."*

Khateeb relates that *Yahya Ibni Maeen* spent more than 1 million *dirhams* until he did not have shoes to wear. *Imam Zahabi* spent 150,000 *dirhams* and *Ali Ibni Aasim* 100,000 *dirhams*. *Ibni Rustum* spent 300,000, and *Hisham* spent 700,000, and not only that but they preserved all that even though they were tortured like *Abu Hanifa, Malik, Shafi*, and *Ahmad*. Then they were careful taking a *hadith*, preserving and delivering it, because many Sahaba only narrate *hadith* a very little. *Ibni Masud* used to become pale while narrating, and *Anas* used to say after narrating,

"Or as the Prophet has said."

Zaid Ibni Arqam did not narrate anything in his old age, because he was afraid, he would miss a word. *Malik* and *Yahya Ibni Saeed* said that we can trust one with hundreds of thousands of *dinars*, but we hardly trust either one regarding narration. *Moeen Ibni Isa* said *Malik* used to listen to a *hadith* 30 times; same was the case of *Ibrahim al Hirawi* from his *Shaikh Hisham*.

Ibrahim Ibni Saeed said,

"If I did not receive a hadith through 100 ways I would think I am an orphan."

This science on one hand is much more important and very difficult as well on the other side. Its preservation is a perpetual miracle of our Prophet.

MAY ALLAH ACCEPT THIS EFFORT, AMIN!

BOOKS BY *QAZI FAZL ULLAH*

Qazi Fazl Ullah has written other books. Below is a brief list with summaries.

FIQH KEE TAREEKH WA IRTIQA (URDU)

Islam is *Deen* (religion) and is a complete code of life. Its laws are of two types, textual and deduced, but how the text is interpreted and how laws are deduced therefrom is called *"Jurisprudence"* and the laws are called *Fiqh,* and how this *Fiqh* got developed and compiled. This book gives the details about its stages of development.

MOHAMMADUR RASOOLULLAH (URDU)

The biography of the *Prophet Mohammad* was preserved from day one by his blessed companions. Then scholars and historians have written books in this regard in various times, both concise and detailed. This book on the biography of *Prophet Mohammad* is an excellent balance of concise and detailed, as a concise a book sometimes misses things, and people do not have time to read and understand too detailed a book. Another important feature of this book is that almost with every important part of the *Prophet's* biography, the relevant part of the *Holy Quran* has been quoted, which illustrates that the *Prophet's* life was the practical shape of the *Holy Book*.

SARMAYA DARANA NIZAM ISHTIRAKIYAT AUR ISLAM *(URDU)*

Humans, throughout their history, have thought ahead and planned their economics and economical needs. They created systems for these purposes. The three systems most widely practiced in history are capitalism, communism, and *Islam*. This book is a comparative study of these 3 economical systems, and it proves that the *Islamic* system bestowed upon us by the Creator is the best one with regard to justice and no room for exploitation.

DAWAT O JIHAD *(URDU)*

The basic duty of every *Prophet* and his followers was and is to call the people towards *Allah* in a peaceful, attractive, and convincing way, and wherever and whenever they encounter resistance and hindrances in this regard, they must remove these hindrances. At times, this leads to fights, as when the conspiracy is big and the opponents try to take away their fundamental rights, so they have the right to defend it but how, when, and where? In this book, it is mentioned that *Islam* teaches us to convey, convince, and convert, but not to coerce. This book is an answer to anti-*Islamic* propaganda, especially about the concept of *Jihad* in *Islam*.

ISLAM AUR SIYASAT (URDU)

Islam and Politics—as it is known from the title that this book discusses *Islamic* political system, because *Islam* is *Deen*, meaning a complete code of life and not a set of a few rituals. It has its own system for state and government. So, wherever *Muslims* are in power, if they will implement this system, they meet the needs of everyone, regardless of color, caste, or religion. *Islam* covers the details, such as how to elect a government, and how to run the state to provide peace and justice to all.

RIYASATI ISLAMI KA TASWWAR
(URDU)

The title means the concept of an *Islamic* state, and *"concept"* means its conduct. In this book, it is mentioned how and why a state and government is needed, and how that state and government may be and should be run. The Creator *Allah* the Almighty knows all our needs, necessities, qualities, and shortcomings, so the system he has given is the only system that can ensure people's security and safety and can provide them peace and justice, making the state a welfare state.

USOOLUT - TAFSEER (ARABIC)

Every branch of science has its own rules, principles, and methodologies, which provide guidelines for explaining it and how to interpret it, so this methodology is a circle or limits one may keep himself confines to, so he will not get lost or go astray.

This book covers the explanation of the *Holy Quran*, the last and final book of *Allah*. The book of *Allah* is the basic source of *Islam* and *Islamic* law, so its explanation requires certain rules to be followed in its explanation, so one may not be unbridled and without restraint, otherwise he will put his faith in danger.

DIRAYATUR RIWAYAH (ARABIC)

Hadith (sayings, actions, and sanctions) of *Prophet Mohammad* is the second fundamental source of *Islam* and *Islamic* laws and also it is the interpretation of the *Holy Quran*. The companions of the *Prophet Mohammad* have preserved them in their memories and in their scriptures and the second and third generation took it from them and preserved them as well. Later on, when there was a fear of perversion, then these *Ahadith* were compiled officially and later on, the authentic scholars gathered them together in various books. Furthermore, critics compiled a biography of all these narrators and put certain rules about how a *Hadith* could be accepted. This book includes all these details.

HUJJIYATI HADITH (URDU)

This book is regarding the authenticity of *Hadith* of the *Prophet*, as there is a baseless propaganda that *Hadith* were not written in the time of the *Prophet*, but later on, making them unreliable. This is wrong, as *Sahaba* used to write *Ahadith* and sometimes the *Prophet* himself used to order them to write. But they trusted their memory more than writing. Official compilation took place later on, when *Muslim* rulers became aware of the weakness of people's memories and the loss of those individuals writing. This book provides all these details and makes it clear that *Hadith* is *Wahi* (Revelation) and source of *Islamic Shariah* (Law).

FUNDAMENTALISM, SECULARISM AUR ISLAM (URDU)

Propaganda is being spread either because of ignorance or with mala fide intention that *Islam* is fundamentalism.

Fundamentalism was a term used for Christianity when it blocked the ways of scientific research, invention and development, and some people wanted to adopt it as a basic guideline for states and government. So those who were with research and development branded that as fundamentalism. But *Islam* does not stop or block progress and research; rather, it encourages it and even orders scholars to go ahead and do research, as discussed in this book.

AL IJTIHADU WAT TAQLEED (URDU)

Humans are social and intellectual animals. They have all the same needs as animals, but they are distinct from them because of their intellect as they are looking for their ease, to do a little and get a lot. For this purpose, some intellectuals invent things and others follow them.

Then as they are bound to obey the *Deen* of *Allah*, there are other intellectuals who deduce laws from its fundamental sources: the *Quran* and the *Sunnah*, and the less intellectuals follow them, as they should. This is the only intellectual and reasonable way. This book explains this issue and its importance.

MUSALMAN AURAT (URDU)

Allah created the world. He created humans and made them men and women. He gave different qualities to both genders for the smooth running of this life to depend upon each other, but as humans they are equal. Some women made history and they did memorable work that many men could not have done. This small book mentions some of the great work of some great women, particularly *Muslim* women, to make it clear that *Islam* deeply respects women and appreciates their contributions to society.

ASMATI RASOOL OR ZAWAJI AAISHA (URDU)

This world is a combination of opposites and some people have been given a great status. The messengers of *Allah* are the chosen and beloved of *Allah*. He made them and built them up for himself and his work. They are the most respected and honored people, and they must be given respect, as any disgrace to them can harm the feelings and sentiments of their followers, which can cause trouble. In this book this issue is discussed, as well as a misconception about the *Prophet's* marriage to *Aaisha*; namely, that she was minor at that time. Academically and research fully, this book corrects this misconception.

AL FARA'ID FIL AQA'ID (ARABIC)

Aqeedah and *Aqa'id* means faith and beliefs, respectively, and they are the base of *Deen*. Certain beliefs are the contents of *Iman*. What is important for a *Muslim* to believe? These are detailed in this concise book. Some *Muslim* sects have misconstrued some of these beliefs, so the book mentions that as well and makes the right faith clear.

QAWA'IDUT - TAJWEED (ARABIC)

One of the basic duties of the *Prophet* was to teach his followers how to recite the holy book properly. His *Sahabah* learnt it from him and then this became a specific science in future generations. They not only taught their students the proper way of recitation, they also wrote books about it. This science is called *Tajweed*, which literally means to make good, but in this science, it means to recite good. This book prescribes the basic rules for *Tajweed* as proper pronunciation not only makes the words and sounds good but also helps in giving the proper meaning of the word.

AL QAWA'IDUL FIQHIYAH (ARABIC)

Islam is *Deen* and a complete system and code of life. For each and every aspect of life there are rules and laws in *Islam*. Some of these rules are in text of the *Quran* and the *Sunnah*, while some others are deduced therefrom. For deduction, the authentic jurists have laid down rules of deduction and the qualities required for themselves. Then, after deduction, they have found some commonalities in different laws in different chapters, so they laid down a common rule for that and these rules called *Al Qawa'idul - Fiqhiyah*, or legal maxims, which make the study of *Fiqh* easy and understandable. This book includes some known and famous legal maxims in all four schools of jurisprudence.

AL JIHAD FIL ISLAM (ARABIC)

Jihad is a very important issue in *Islam*; to defend life, property, honor, and faith is not only a well-known right in each and every culture but also a duty in *Islam*, but how and when? This book is written on this subject; and as this issue is quite controversial, this is a reasonable answer to these questions in the light of the *Quran* and *Sunnah*.

MAULANA UBAIDULLAH SINDHI (URDU)

Maulana Ubaid Ullah Sindhi, originally from a *Sikh* family, accepted *Islam* when he was a teenager. He studied *Deen* in the proper and traditional way, then joined the freedom movement. He went through a lot of difficulties and lived in exile for 24 years. As a revolutionary leader, he is controversial, and many people wrote against him as well as for him. This book describes his personality, struggle, and thoughts to know who he was and how he was.

ASMATI RASOOL AND KHATMI NUBUWWAT (URDU)

Asmati Rasool and *Khatmi Nubuwwat* are reasonable and logical. This book consists of two parts. The defense of the *Prophet* and that of him being the last and final *Prophet* of *Allah* is a reasonable and logical thing, as *Allah* sent messengers in different times to different areas and different nations, and when they worked in their respected times in those areas, *Allah* sent the *Prophet Mohammad* to the entire world to combine their work and bring humanity together on the same theme, subject and faith that all those earlier messengers were sent for. This book is a concise, detailed, and logical interpretation of this finality.

SAYYIDAH AAISHA'S AGE AT MARRIAGE (ENGLISH)

Islam is a Natural *Deen* or *Deen* of Nature. This is a balanced *Deen* providing a comprehensive justice system, and the *Holy Prophet* is the perfect role model as a perfect human. His words, actions, and sanctions are the proper interpretation of the *Holy Quran* and the second fundamental source of laws in *Islam*. There is a commonly held belief, especially among critics of *Islam*, that the *Prophet* married *Aaisha* when she was only nine years of age. In this book, all the details about this issue are given that how this word *Tis'aa* (which means nine) happened there and what the real story is to counter the false accounts and correct the record.

JIHAD IN ISLAM: WHY, HOW, AND WHEN? (ENGLISH)

Jihad as a word in *Arabic* means struggle or striving hard, especially for a noble cause, while as a term in *Islam*, it specifically means to fight in the path/cause of *Allah*. But when does this fight happen? When it is inevitable and unavoidable as the very integrity of a state, the lives of its citizens or the very ideology is facing a big danger. But a very baseless smear campaign is going on against *Jihad* and it is branded as a synonym to terrorism, so this book is a must to make the true concept of *Jihad* clear and counter the propaganda.

SHARIA AND POLITICS (ENGLISH)

Islam is *Deen* and *Deen* means a complete system and a perfect code of life as this is given by the very creator of the worlds, who knows all about his creatures, their qualities, and their shortcomings, and can provide a perfect solution to their problems. But unfortunately, some people have been doing wrong in the name of *Khalafat* and presenting their wrong idea as the *Islamic* political system, so there was great need of a book that can present the proper shape of an *Islamic* state and *Islamic* political system given by the Creator; when executed properly, it is actually a mercy and blessing for the creatures. This book explains this concept clearly.

HAJJ & UMRAH IN ALL FOUR SCHOOLS OF JURISPRUDENCE (ENGLISH)

Hajj (pilgrimage to *Mecca*) is one of the Five Pillars of *Islam* and an especially important but a complicated type of *Ibadah* (worship) as

Muslims from all around the world get together to perform it together. They follow the interpretation of their *Imams* (jurists), sometimes they look at others when they do not perform a specific virtue the way they do, then they think they are doing wrong, which is not so, but all of them are performing correctly according to the interpretation of their *Imams*. This book gives all these details in sequence according to all four *Imams* the *Muslim Ummah* follows.

RAMADAN: COMPONENTS OF THE HOLY MONTH (ENGLISH)

The *Islamic* Calendar is lunar based. It's different *Ibadaat* time is based on moonsighting; the lunar month starts with the new moon. Even though astronomy tells us what day the moon will be born (i.e., new) with perfect accuracy, discerning on which day it will be visible in a specific area is still not accurate. That is why differences in opinion happen all over the world, and should we to go by the calendar or by a sighting?

Also, at *Ramadan*, which is the most important month in *Islam* as a mandatory *Ibadah*, fasting is mandatory as well, but there is an extra, highly recommended *Ibadah*, the *Taraweeh*, but how many *Rakat* should we pray? *Muslims* differ about this. Another important *Ibadah* is *Salat Ul Witr*. We use this prayer all year, but during *Ramadan* this is prayed in *Jama'at*, and different *Imams* have different opinions regarding the number of *Rakats* and its procedure. So, this book gives all the details about these three prominent issues.

SCIENCE OF HADITH (ENGLISH)

Hadith is the second fundamental source of *Islamic* law. They are the words, actions, and sanctions of the *Holy Prophet*. To record all these in memory and writing, to compile it and to record the biography of those narrators who did this great job, and this is considered as a miracle of the *Prophet*. But the enemies of *Islam* used to create doubts in this regard. This book is written on this subject, and it is enough an answer to all the objections that people made from different angles.

HAJJ & UMRAH IN ALL FOUR SCHOOLS OF JURISPRUDENCE (URDU)

Hajj (pilgrimage to *Mecca*) is one of the Five Pillars of *Islam* and an especially important but a complicated type of *Ibadah* (worship) as *Muslims* from all around the world get together to perform it together. They follow the interpretation of their *Imams* (jurists), sometimes they look at others when they do not perform a specific virtue the way they do, then they think they are doing wrong, which is not so, but all of them are performing correctly according to the interpretation of their *Imams*. This book gives all these details in sequence according to all four *Imams* the *Muslim Ummah* follows.

USOOL AT - TAFSEER (PASHTO)

Every branch of science has its own rules, principles, and methodologies, which provide guidelines for explaining it and how to interpret it, so this methodology is a circle or limits one may keep himself confines to, so he will not get lost or go astray.

This book covers the explanation of the *Holy Quran*, the last and final book of *Allah*. The book of *Allah* is the basic source of *Islam* and *Islamic* law, so its explanation requires certain rules to be followed in its explanation, so one may not be unbridled and without restraint, otherwise he will put his faith in danger.

BIDAYATUL FUHUL FI ILMIL USOOL *(ARABIC)*

Islamic Fiqh is "shariah" or laws of Islam. Laws are of two types substantive and procedural and all of these laws are based upon jurisprudence. "Ilmul Usool" which is called "Ilmul Fiqh" also is the jurisprudence of "shariah." As we know that in Islam there are four famous schools of jurisprudence. i.e. Hanafi, Maliki, Shafi, Hanbali. In this book the jurisprudence of all these schools are explained which can be useful for those who are interested in it. It will help them know how imams differ on certain issues.

KHUDA KAHA HAY? *(URDU)*

Allah placed his concept in human nature. Throughout human history people believed in Allah in one way or the other. Even agnostics as they bewilder like one who is looking for something. The atheists deny him but their denial is actually an admission that something exists but deny it. Muslims believe in Allah but there are certain issues they differ in. Its proper interpretation as to whether Allah is on the throne or is everywhere. In this book we tried to bring forth both concepts along with its proper expression as to what they meant by both.

USOOL AT - TAFSEER (URDU)

Every branch of science has its own rules, principles, and methodologies, which provide guidelines for explaining it and how to interpret it, so this methodology is a circle or limits one may keep himself confines to, so he will not get lost or go astray.

This book covers the explanation of the *Holy Quran*, the last and final book of *Allah*. The book of *Allah* is the basic source of *Islam* and *Islamic* law, so its explanation requires certain rules to be followed in its explanation, so one may not be unbridled and without restraint, otherwise he will put his faith in danger.

MOHAMMAD THE APOSTLE OF MERCY (ENGLISH)

The biography of the *Prophet Mohammad* was preserved from day one by his blessed companions. Then scholars and historians have written books in this regard in various times, both concise and detailed. This book on the biography of *Prophet Mohammad* is an excellent balance of concise and detailed, as a concise a book sometimes misses things, and people do not have time to read and understand too detailed a book. Another important feature of this book is that almost with every important part of the *Prophet's* biography, the relevant part of the *Holy Quran* has been quoted, which illustrates that the *Prophet's* life was the practical shape of the *Holy Book*.

AHSAN UL KALAM FIL A'IMMATIL AALAM (URDU)

Allah has created the world as and created therein different creatures. He created mankind as his *Khalifa* i.e. agent. He gave mankind the talent to exploit the world and the resources therein for their good, but at the same time he made him bound to follow his orders and commands. These are meant to make the life in this world a content one and prosperous in the hereafter. Allah sent mankind messengers, prophets, and books at different times. Prophet Mohammad was sent as the final messenger with the Holy Quran which he explained with words and actions. But as nature is evolutionary and the world is ephemeral which changes constantly so new issues emerge which needs solutions, so in his followers Allah blessed certain people with specific knowledge of Quran and Sunnah. They deduce and further explain these for people. These blessed people were few in number but the juristic work of four of them namely *Abu Hanifa, Malek, Shafi,* and *Ahmad* was compiled properly. These are valuable assets of Islam and majority of *ummah* do follow these four jurists all over the world since their time till now.

This book *Ahsan Ul Kalam Fil A'immatil Aalam* is an introduction of these great jurists and their work in brief.

BAHLOL DANA AIK MU'AMMA SHAKHSIYAT (URDU)

Bahlol Dana is the nickname of Amr Ibni Wahab Al Kufi. He was a scholar from the Hashimite tribe. To avoid the post of judge he pretended not to be in his senses. He frequently visited Khalifa Harun and Mamun and would advise them their ministers. He would relay the issues faced by the common people and how best to address them.

He was a clever and talented individual. His lectures and words are golden but have never been compiled in a singular place according to our research. They are scattered through ought many books and we tried our best to compile them in order to gain the wisdom therein.

All those who studied the book, enjoyed its content and. The Prophet said *"the word of wisdom is the lost assets of a wise man, he deserves that wherever he found it."* So this is a word of wisdom.

IQNA -US SAAIL FI THALATHI MASA'IL (URDU)

As Muslims we are bound to worship Allah the way we have been taught and shown by the prophet Mohammad. This worship is *Fard*, *Wajib*, *Sunnah* and *Mustalab*. For certain *Ibadaat* there is a specific time and way they are to be performed. Among these *Ibadaat* prayer is the utmost important *Ibadah* and *Ramadan* is the utmost important time for *Ibadaat*.

As the lunar month starts with moon sighting and an extra ordinarily recommended prayer *Taraweeh* taking place nightly for the entire month. This prayer includes *Salati Wit'r* in congregation. In this book we have attempted to explain these three issues in the light of *Quran* and sunnah. Means 1- Moon sighting 2- *Salat Ul Taraweeh* 3- *Salat Ul Wit'r*. May *Allah* accept this effort. Ameen

ASMATI I RASOOL KHATMI NUBUWWAT AQLI AUR MANTIQI HAY (URDU)

Allah (swt) made humans bound to obey his commandments and follow his rules. For the said purpose he sent the messengers as teachers and role models. A role model has to be perfect and these he made them "maasoom" (protected). He sent Prophet Mohammad as his last and final prophet to the whole world until the last day. Allah made the Prophet extra ordinally perfect role model and ordered us to believe him as such. We are to protect and defend his finality as this is logical and reasonable.

This book is regarding this important fundamental issue. Herein this is explained logically, reasonably and textually. May Allah accept this effort. Amin!

KHULAFA E RASHIDEEN (URDU)

ABOUT THE AUTHOR

Qazi Fazl Ullah is an American philosopher, linguist, and author. He is *Fazil Wafaqul Madaris* where he studied *Arabic* grammar, *Arabic* literature, *Fiqh*, jurisprudence, logic, philosophy, *Ilmul Kalam, Seerah, Tafseer, Hadith,* and *Islamic* history. He studied at *Peshawar University* and *Islamic University Islamabad* in *Pakistan* and specialized in law, economics, and political science. He has taught all these subjects in *Pakistan* and the United States at different institutions. He was elected as a *National Assembly Parliamentarian* in *Pakistan*. He worked in underserved areas to provide jobs, build infrastructure, schools, museums, public health facilities, and increase communication technologies as the chair of the *Social Action Board*. He has traveled extensively throughout the Middle East, North Africa, Europe, Southeast Asia, North and Central America. He has given seminars in various parts of the world in these subjects. He speaks and has given lectures and seminars in *Urdu, Pashto, Farsi,* English, and *Arabic*. He has published works in *Pashto, Urdu, Arabic,* and English internationally. He has given the complete *Tafsir Ul Quran* in *Pashto* multiple times in *Pakistan*. He has also given *Tafsir Ul Quran* in *Urdu, Pashto,* and English in the United States. It includes *Usul Ul Fiqh, Usul Ul Mirath, Hadith al Qudsi, Hadith an Nabawi* in English on multiple occasions. He considers himself a student to continue acquisition of knowledge. He is currently leading *Tafsir Ul Quran, Usual Al Fiqh, Seerat Un Nabi,* Science of Inheritance (*Mirath*) in English and *Al Mukhtar Lil Fatawa, Dirayat Ul Riwaya* in *Arabic* in Los Angeles, California.

www.ingramcontent.com/pod-product-compliance
Lightning Source LLC
Chambersburg PA
CBHW030310100426
42812CB00002B/653